It Takes Cow Chips to Make Dinner

by L. Dale Redlin

Illustrated by Abby Matzke

IN THANKFUL MEMORY
of
Ma and Pa who provided
a loving Christian home for their
children and worked very
hard to support their
family under difficult
circumstances

Erben House, LLC
www.erbenhouse.com
info@erbenhouse.com
1521 N Argonne Rd, Suite C221
Spokane Valley, WA 99212

Illustrations by Abby Matzke
Photo credit: back cover and page iii, from the L. Dale Redlin personal archive
Cover photo: © 2025 Nicole Free

ISBN 979-8-9865934-2-5

Printed in the United States of America
Second edition

Table of Episodes

Preface

The Purpose

My memories of growing up during the thirties and forties in rural South Dakota are still very vivid in my mind. As I consciously tried to recall certain happenings in order to record them, I found that the reality of those days began to flood my memory with details that had evidently lay latent for many years. I found myself reliving those days with fondness, excitement, joy, sadness, and sometimes even tears.

My purpose for recording some of my memories from those years is to demonstrate to the present generation, especially to my grandchildren, that there was another time when things were very different. Many of the things that we take for granted today were not so much as heard of in those days. But life went on with little or no complaining. Life went on with a joyful and thankful spirit. Life went on with a closeness, especially among family. Yes, life went on, without electricity, plumbing, insurance; with hardly enough means to buy groceries; sometimes without a car and sometimes without a home. Amazingly, through it all, my memories are mostly good and happy.

Some, whom I forced to listen to stories from my past, seemed to enjoy them. (Now that I think about it, perhaps they simply were being polite.) Nevertheless, it seemed that in my retirement I could begin to record a few of the happenings that took place some 70 years before. In that way, I would have an excuse to relive some of those fond memories of the "good ol' days."

No doubt some of you who read these pages will be able to relate to the episodes quite readily. Some of the special characters mentioned will remind you of people whom you know or knew. There was no need to fictionalize. Real people from my life have always provided all of the entertainment and challenges necessary to keep life interesting.

The Title

The title of this little book comes from one of my regular chores. I was the official cow chip gatherer. Ma was talking to me when she called out with that never-to-be-forgotten announcement, *"I need cow chips to make dinner!"* This, in itself, serves as a glance into life in those years, especially in rural South Dakota.

Ma had a cow chip box on the porch. As a five-year-old, it was my job to keep it full. Ma always wore gloves when she carried the box of cow chips into the kitchen. She opened the lids on the big four-lidded cook stove and put some crumpled up paper in first. Then she carefully broke some chips and placed them over the paper and lit it. Ma quickly closed the lid and soon the fire was roaring. More chips were added and soon the stove was hot. The water in the reservoir began to bubble and steam. The potatoes began to cook in the cooker and meat began to crackle and sizzle in the hot grease in the frying pan. Soon dinner was ready!

I felt some satisfaction that I could contribute to making dinner. I didn't know anything about cooking, but I did know how to gather cow chips! They needed to be seasoned, sun-dried, mature chips, at least a month old. Those were the best: easy to handle, odorless, and loaded with energy. So when the chip box was nearly empty, Ma called out with words that are indelibly fixed in my memory to this day, *"I need cow chips to make dinner!"*

Those were much simpler times. The episodes, as I recall them, are a humble attempt to picture briefly for my grandchildren and eventually, perhaps, my great-grandchildren (and any one else who might find them worth reading), the life and times of another generation. Perhaps—just perhaps—this small volume may play some small role in helping future generations appreciate a bit more the many blessings that we enjoy today but so easily take for granted. And, by the way, we did walk more than a mile to school—up hill both ways!

> With thankful remembrances
> of days gone by,
>
> L. Dale Redlin

Joe

Neighbors watched out for each other in the rural areas of South Dakota. If they didn't notice some activity in the neighbor's yard or in the field for a time, a visit was in order. However, winter was a more difficult time to stay in touch. The outdoor activity, generally, was severely limited due to snow and cold temperatures. Nevertheless, there was always the sleigh and horses.

We hadn't seen Joe for some time. He lived about a mile from our place. Pa became concerned. One day in the dead of winter, Pa asked me a question to which he knew the answer. He asked anyway, "How about going for a sleigh ride?"

Of course, I was always up for that. "Sure," I answered, "Where are we going?"

"You'll see," Pa replied, rather mysteriously. So Pa and I bundled up, hitched up the horses to our sleigh, and took off through the deep snow.

As the matching black Percherons trotted obediently in synchronized fashion, the sleigh bells chimed

in melodic rhythm. Pa bent over and whispered, as though not to interrupt the moment, "We're going to visit Joe."

Joe was a bachelor. We wondered how he made a living. He farmed a few acres, but he was a very poor farmer. Today, farmers speak of no-till farming. Well, Joe was way ahead of his time. Every year, he scratched the soil a little with his team of horses pulling an old field cultivator. He planted the seed with his even older wood and rusty metal grain drill. Then he pulled a wooden drag with metal spikes across the field to try to cover the seed with soil. Most of the time the wind blew the shallow covering of earth off the seed and the birds had a hearty feast. Yet, amazingly, if we were blessed with rain at just the right time, some of the seed sprouted and grew. Joe often had a crop to harvest. Sort of! The neighbors always helped Joe harvest. He used the little grain he harvested to feed his few chickens, two milk cows, and a couple of pigs.

We covered our faces with our scarves as we headed into the frigid north wind. Tiny icicles formed on our scarves as the air froze our breath. The horses grew white "whiskers" as their breath steamed from their nostrils. All was peaceful and quiet. Only the soft sound of the sleigh runners knifing through the snow and the sleigh bells ringing in strict cadence broke the silence of this brisk winter day. Wildlife was scarce, but we did spot a big jack rabbit racing with us a few yards away and suddenly flushing a rooster pheasant from his grassy, snow-covered igloo.

As we drew closer, we saw smoke curling from the chimney of Joe's tiny house, signaling that likely he was safe and sound. We tied the horses to a post and knocked on the door. After much rustling and what sounded like sliding furniture, finally, Joe opened the door. "Well, hello," Joe grunted in a rather coarse, raspy voice. "Come on in."

Joe was a short, squatty fellow in his mid-fifties. At least a month's growth of graying whiskers covered his plump cheeks and chin. His bib-overalls were well worn and grimy. His tattered flannel shirt, buttoned tight up to the neck, needed washing. His hairless head was covered by his winter cap.

Joe's three-room house was dark and gloomy. The wooden floor was well worn, dirty, and squeaked when we walked on it. We were surprised at how extremely warm it was in his house.

As we proceeded to remove our overshoes Joe urged, "Don't bother. A little snow won't make any difference." He was right, of course. We removed them anyway and put them together with our coats on the floor beside the door. As we did so, Pa noticed a very large, new pair of overshoes sitting there. Surprised, Pa remarked, "Joe, looks like you bought a new pair of overshoes."

"Ya," Joe replied, "they cost too much." Joe came over and proudly held them up. "Paid a dollar forty-nine for 'em."

They were really big! Pa couldn't help but ask, "Joe, why are they so big? You don't wear that size overshoes, do you?"

Joe paused a bit and then put the overshoes back on the floor. "No, Levi," he answered, "I wear size nine. But you know, I thought at a dollar forty-nine I should get all I could for my money. I bought the biggest pair I could get. These are size 14!" Pa looked at me with a mischievous grin but never said a word.

"Come in by the stove," Joe invited. We were already roasting, but we politely followed Joe into his "living room." No wonder it was hot with the strong smell of smoke in the air! The pot-bellied stove door was wide open! Joe had perched a ten-foot log on two chairs. The end of the log went through the open door of the big pot-bellied stove. The fire was blazing away. We stood for a moment without any one of us saying a word. Then Joe volunteered, in his perfectly reasonable way, "This is my new way of burning wood. Why should I spend all my time and energy cutting and splitting it? This works just fine." As we sat with Joe for about an hour, he only had to move the log one time. Maybe it was a good idea after all. A large puff of smoke, now and then, ascending up to the ceiling, seemed to go totally unnoticed by Joe.

Pa and Joe talked about the weather and farming and how to kill rats in the cellar. The cellars under many of the houses were nothing but a hole in the ground. Sometimes there were steps, but often just a ladder, down into the dark, damp, black hole in the ground. Usually, there were no windows in the foundation of the house, so one needed a lantern to go down into this dismal, musty den, which nobody liked. Rats were a constant pest in the cellars where food was usually stored for the winter.

Pa ventured to help Joe with his rat problem. Pa's tried and tested solution was this: "Joe, why don't you take a deep bucket and put about eight inches of water in it. Put the bucket in the cellar and I'll bet you'll get results. When the rats get thirsty they will try to reach the water. It is out of their reach so they will slip, fall into the water, and drown."

All was silent. Joe continued to stare into the fire and said nothing for awhile. "Will that work?" he finally responded.

"It works for me," Pa answered.

Joe sat silently as though analyzing Pa's solution. "But what do you do when you get two or three dead rats in the bucket?" Joe inquired with a puzzled look.

Pa answered with the obvious answer, "You have to carry them out and dump them. In the spring you can bury them."

Again, Joe was silent for a time as he continued to stare into the fire in deep thought, apparently mulling over Pa's final statement. Finally, after what seemed like a couple of minutes, Joe abruptly answered, "No, Levi, that's way too much work." Well, that was the end of that rather penetrating discussion.

After about an hour, we were both hot and sweating. Nevertheless, we bundled up for the cold ride home. We admired Joe's size 14 overshoes one last time and headed out the door and back to the patiently waiting horses and the sleigh for the rather brisk ride home. We were thankful that Joe was in good spirits, healthy, and typically Joe.

The horses seemed to welcome heading for home. As they lurched effortlessly through the snow banks, Pa chuckled and commented, "Joe is one of a kind. He could probably walk all over his yard without his overshoes ever moving."

The Ol' Sand Pit

Every child needs a place to go to let his mind wander and his imagination soar: a place to dream and discover. My place was the ol' sand pit. This special place was the "graveyard" for all sorts of things that people threw away. To most people it was a junk pit, but for my brother and me it was a treasure land full of surprises. Our toys came from the ol' sand pit, and I'm sure that we enjoyed them at least as much as the children who received them the first time around when they were all new and shiny and when everything worked!

For many months, I had paged through the Montgomery Ward catalog, always turning to the section where the wagons were displayed. I looked and dreamed and wondered if I would ever have one of my own. It seemed like a hopeless dream. But what fun I had coasting and hauling things in my day-dreams. So you can probably imagine what joy I felt when there— in the ol' sand pit—among some junk—we saw a handle of a wagon and a corner of the box.

We dug and moved old wire, tin cans, moldy mattresses, and various other things, until we uncovered

this old, paintless, rusty wagon box. It had a handle and running gear, but the wheels were nowhere around. No matter! It held possibilities—a real Chitty Chitty Bang Bang, if you know what I mean! Excitedly, we dragged it home. For a number of days, after we finished our chores, we went to the ol' sand pit searching for any "new things." But now, mostly, we were hunting for wheels for our wagon.

One by one, we uncovered and discovered what were, to us, precious surprises. We found one wheel, then another. Matching wheels! They were without tires and small. Not a problem. We hunted day after day. Finally, after a few days, we found two larger wheels, one with a tire the other without. The small wheels went on the front and the large ones on the rear.

What a hot rod! Low in the front and high in the rear. We found some wire to insert in the hole in the axle to hold the wheels on and we were all set. Finally, we had a wagon. And it worked, even though it wobbled a lot. What a great help for gathering cow chips and doing other chores. It even worked for coasting down a hill and for pulling and pushing each other around the yard. Fun, fun, fun!

At a very young age I learned the essence of what someone wisely once said, "The happiest people don't necessarily have the best of everything, they just make the best of everything they have."

My Friend the Steamer

Wheeeho—Wheeeho! The air horn of the steam engine crisply pierced the early morning hours. I dropped my spoon and left the breakfast table to rush outside and wave at my friend the steamer. The railroad track of the Great Northern Railway ran about 200 yards from our house. It was a steam engine with a loud air horn. Sometimes the engineer blew the horn as it went by. We always tried to respond with a wave.

Some may think that with the railroad running so close to our home we must have had a terribly noisy, dirty place to live. Well, they would be right. The black and gray smoke pouring from the smokestack often drifted directly across our house. When the wind was from the direction of the railroad, Ma never washed clothes to be hung on the clothesline to dry. But there were some advantages.

The train engine was a steam engine, so that meant it used fuel to heat the water. The water became steam, and the steam, under pressure, ran the engine. The fuel was coal. Behind the engine there was a coal car. The fireman had the job of refueling the firebox of the engine. With his shovel he threw the coal into the firebox. Did he always hit his target? I'm afraid not! As a matter of fact, from time to time, apparently, the fireman missed the fire chamber entirely. The coal fell between the cars onto the track below. We just couldn't let that coal go to waste. Right? It was a rather rare commodity at our place. So, whose job was it to pick up the coal that had fallen on the tracks? Of course, it was mine!

My Uncle Ed helped me. He lived with us for some time. Though mentally and physically challenged, Ed helped with odd jobs. So now and then, Ed and I walked up and down the railroad tracks and gathered the coal. Uncle Ed was my "pack horse" equipped with an old newspaper bag that he carried across his shoulder. He and I had a good time finding the coal and filling the bag. When the bag became too heavy for Uncle Ed to carry I fetched—you guessed it—my little rusty wagon. Ed dumped the coal into the wagon. Finally, when we had a wagonload we proudly hauled the coal home for a more permanent fire in the cook stove. If we had a good year, we might have gathered enough coal to help fire the old pot-bellied stove in the corner of the living room when winter came.

The train became a real part of our lives. Noisy?
Yes. Dirty? Yes. But the powerful choo-choo, choo-
choo, the friendly engineer, the brakeman riding on
the back of the caboose waving to us, the curiosity of
what the cargo was each time, and that wonderfully
loud, shrill whistle—it all became part of our lives. The
train, with all its faults, became a close friend and a
daily companion.

Goin' Fishin'

"Let's go fishin'," Pa invited. I knew exactly what he meant. Excitedly, I ran to get my "fishing gear." What kind of fishing gear did I have? It was nothing more than a washtub and my little ol' rusty wagon. Pa went to the barn to get his "gear." He didn't have a fishing pole. He had one once, but he was too impatient to sit and wait for a fish to bite so he threw it in the river and never had one again. Pa's "fishing pole" was a pitchfork. He used it around the barn for pitching straw and hay. At threshing time he used it for pitching bundles. And when it was time for fishing he used it to "catch" fish. Kind of a multi-purpose "fishing pole."

We walked together across the pasture down to the Sioux River that flowed about two hundred yards beyond our barn. Each spring the water became very deep in the river. We waited until the river had become rather shallow—about one and a half to two feet deep. We could see the dorsal fins of the big carp and buffalo surfacing from time to time. That was Pa's kind of fishing.

18

It was a beautiful setting. Cattle were grazing in the green pasture. Our team of slick, black draft horses romped and kicked in the summer sun. Meadow larks were singing their hearts out from the tops of fence posts. Robins were here and there, tugging on worms that they managed to find in the soft earth not far from the river's edge. The red-winged blackbirds were perched in the marsh grass singing their typical squeaky Akong-ka-ree. It was a good day for fishin'.

Pa rolled up his pants to above his knees. He did that not to keep them from getting wet. He knew he was going to get wet. He rolled up his pants so that he could walk more easily in the water. He took the fork and began to wade into the river's edge, watching for a sign of a fish. He walked slowly, trying not to spook the fish and also carefully trying to avoid any holes, slippery stones, rusty cans, or broken glass on the bottom.

I was always excited when we went fishing. I couldn't see the fish from the bank but I watched Pa. Suddenly, he plunged the fork into the water, pushing it all the way to the bottom of the river. He held it for a few seconds. If he felt a fish squirming under the fork, then he knew he had one. He waited a while longer. Soon the water turned red with blood around the fork. Pa carefully lifted the fish up high above his head and threw it up on the bank. Now, my job began. My appointed duty was to grab the slippery, slimy, wiggly, bloody fish and somehow get it into the wash tub.

Usually they were big fish. Pa said they weighed from ten to fifteen pounds. Sometimes Pa just stopped and laughed as I struggled with one of those slippery critters. But I had my laughs too. Pa's carefulness didn't always help. Splash! Pa was down in the water, struggling to regain his footing. He either stepped in a hole or slipped on a rock, and down into the water he went. Then I got my turn to laugh as Pa finally found his footing came up gasping, sputtering, and laughing.

With our fish in the washtub, we walked together back to the house laughing and talking about some of the happenings of our "fishing trip." Pa was soaking wet. I was usually wet, slimy, and bloody. But we were happy. I can still hear Pa saying, "Now, that's what I call good fishin'!" Pa field-cleaned and scaled them. The rest was up to Ma.

Poor Ma! She did all the hard work. If we "caught" a lot of fish, Ma had to figure out how to process them to preserve them. Of course, we had no refrigerator, not even an icebox. Some were fried and eaten immediately. Some were canned and some were given to neighbors and friends. But none went to waste! Pa said more than once, "There is no better meal than a platter of fried fish, a loaf of homemade bread, and a pound of butter. Nothing else!" Now that I think about it, it's hard to argue with that.

Doctor Brown

It was such a clean, sterile and healthy-looking place. There was a strange odor lingering in the air. The men all wore white coats. The ladies were dressed in crisp, white dresses with perky little white, queen-like crowns.

I had never been to a hospital before. In fact, I was not even at a hospital when I was born. I was born at home. That was the first time I met Dr. Brown, even though I didn't know it. My oldest brother remembered the day very well. He filled me in on all the details. I was about to be born. Ma was finishing some chores in the kitchen when she turned to Pa and calmly announced, "I think it's time. Maybe you should go and get Dr. Brown." Of course, we didn't have a telephone, so Pa drove in to town to fetch the Doctor.

Dr. Brown was not in any hurry. When he finally arrived with his nurse, much had to be done. But Dr. Brown seemed unconcerned. He made himself comfortable in one of our living room chairs while the nurse busily made all of the preparations. Time passed.

Dr. Brown fell fast asleep. I decided to come into the world. The nurse took care of everything marvelously well. There were no complications.

Immediately, Ma asked, "Is it a boy or a girl?"

"A boy," the nurse announced. Well, that was sort of unexpected. Up until that time, my siblings had followed a pattern: Boy—girl—boy—girl—boy—oops, boy. But Ma was happy that I was perfectly healthy. The nurse finished her work and came out of the bedroom. She noticed that Dr. Brown was "sleeping like a log." She nudged him and he inquired groggily, "How is everything?" She assured him that all was well. "Good job," he congratulated as he picked up his coat, hat, and doctor's bag, which he hadn't opened. He turned to Pa and said, "That will be twenty-five dollars." Pa handed the doctor five dollars and promised to pay the rest as soon as possible. Dr. Brown assured Pa that was perfectly okay. He shook Pa's hand, opened the door to the bedroom, congratulated Ma, and left.

Now, I was about five years old and found myself walking down this long hall tagging along behind Ma and Pa and my sister, Viola. I asked Ma, "What is that smell?" Ma told me that it was ether. I asked, "What do they use that for?"

She briefly explained, "They use it to put people to sleep before performing surgery." I didn't know what surgery was but I didn't ask. *That's something that I won't have to think about anyway,* I thought to myself.

Ma and Pa had brought my sister in to the hospital because she often had a sore throat. Dr. Brown had told them to bring her in to have her tonsils removed. "It won't take very long," Dr. Brown had promised. So as he led my sister down the hall he assured Ma and Pa, "I'll have her out of here in a couple of hours." He was right. In less than two hours, my sister came out of the door at the end of the long hall. She seemed rather unsteady as she walked toward us and appeared rather pale and sick, but no one seemed alarmed.

Then I got the shock of my life. Dr. Brown came over to where I was sitting and said, "You're next!" *Next for what?* I wondered. He said, "Just come with me."

I looked up to Ma and Pa. Pa assured me, "It's okay. You can go with the doctor."

Dr. Brown, in his white suit and cap, reached out and took my hand. "Come with me young man," he spoke reassuringly. I was scared. What I didn't know was that Dr. Brown had discussed the matter with Pa previously. He had told Pa that a number of young student physicians were to be visiting at the hospital. He suggested that he would remove my tonsils without charge if Pa would give permission. He had convinced Pa that tonsils were a rather useless organ that we are better off without. Dr. Brown had chosen me for this special assignment because he wanted to give the young students a first-hand basic lesson in removing tonsils without having to be concerned with infections or other complications. I was a perfect candidate. I was healthy, and my tonsils were healthy too!

Soon I was in the operating room and on that hard operating table. I had this big knot in my stomach but I didn't know what to do. I wanted to cry but I tried to be brave. The nurse gently covered my body with a clean white sheet. She carefully tucked it in around my neck. She spoke softly and kindly assured me, "Everything will be just fine."

What I had smelled in the hallway was now very strong. *Is this what surgery is?* I thought to myself. The kind nurse instructed, "Now, Dale, I want you to count to ten out loud and then begin to count again." I was thinking, *I'm sure glad that my sister taught me how to count. If she hadn't, I would really be in trouble!* A large cotton cloth with that smelly stuff, ether, was placed over my nose and I counted to ten. Then again: one, two...three...four...five...six...seven...

The next thing I knew, I was waking up with a very sore throat. I felt sick. I asked, "Why do I feel so sick?"

"You have swallowed a large amount of blood," the nurse explained.

"A lot of blood?" I blurted out. I learned that the doctor had taken more time than usual. He wanted to make sure that the students had a good lesson in removing tonsils. So he took his time. While he carefully taught his students, I was swallowing my own blood. *How gross is that?* I thought to myself.

The nice nurse assured me, "You will feel better tomorrow." That afternoon I was bundled up and my sister and I were helped into the sleigh and we rode home. The nurse was right. I did feel a bit better the next day. I stayed in the house a number of days waiting for my throat to heal. I ate mostly potato soup and drank warm cocoa with home-made buttered bread dipped in the cocoa. Mmmmmm good!

Today, doctors know that healthy tonsils are very helpful and function as a God-given part of our body which is wonderfully made. But when I was young, they were thought to be an unnecessary nuisance. At least I learned to know what ether was for and what surgery was all about.

A Lot-a-Bull

The summer breezes gently caressed the meadows. A sea of green grass with pretty wildflowers beckoned me to enjoy the wonders of God's creation. As a little boy, everything was a wonder. There were the gophers darting through the grass toward their homes in the ground and the meadow larks singing their refrain which my older siblings had verbalized into a musical, "Wash your mother's table cloth," or the not so nice, "I see teacher's petty coat." There were the garter snakes slithering through the grass in search of a meal and the frogs croaking at the river's edge. The butterflies were darting from one weed to another and the bees were searching each flower for nectar.

On this particular day, I became lost in the wonders of nature. I wandered far from our house into the meadows adjoining our homestead. I was so busy chasing gophers that I hadn't noticed our neighbor's herd of cattle grazing in the open, fenceless meadows just ahead. Then, just as a jack rabbit jumped up from his hiding place and hopped away, I raised my eyes to see the neighbor's cattle not far from where I was. This did

27

not alarm me immediately because I was acquainted with cattle. I helped Uncle Ed herd our milk cows wherever there was good grazing, and I was often around the barn.

I stood there for a short time studying the tiny calves as they wobbled along beside their mothers. Here and there, I watched as calves decided to have a midday snack. Their mothers readily obliged. What I hadn't noticed at first, soon became quite apparent. Out of the herd of cattle came a huge reddish-brown bull. His white head was framed with huge, curved horns. He held his head high and began walking quickly and firmly in my direction. My heart sank and began to beat more quickly. I turned and began to half-walk and half-run toward home. I glanced over my shoulder. The big red bull was picking up his pace. He shook his huge head, snorted, and focused directly upon me. His eyes looked glassy and penetrating.

I started to run. The bull began to trot more quickly. Now I was running as fast as I could in the uneven pasture. I tripped over a gopher mound and fell full-length into a very fresh cow pie! But that was the least of my worries. My breathing became more difficult as my chest began to tighten. I got to my feet and quickly glanced over my shoulder. He paused for a minute. Then he began to snort, pawing the ground with his front hooves, throwing the dirt and grass high in the air. He stopped—stared for a moment—then once again he was trotting in my direction.

I ran as fast as I could. With my mouth wide open, my breathing became a wheezing sound. I was sure that this would further aggravate the bull, but I couldn't help it. I wanted to call out for Ma but I knew that she wouldn't hear me. Even if she could hear me, what would she be able to do? Tears of fear were running

down my cheeks as I finally entered our yard. I stumbled up the porch steps and fell into Ma's arms, fresh cow manure and all. I was wheezing and crying and pointing toward the door. Ma went to the door and looked out. There, at the edge of our yard, stood the big red bull proudly holding his head high staring directly at the house. After his victorious moment, he turned and trotted back to the herd. He had protected his harem.

"Oh," Ma cried, "Thank God you're safe!"

That night I said a special prayer to God, thanking Him for watching over me and keeping me safe from that big red bull. I also was thankful for Ma who took care of everything without so much as a scolding. She knew that I had learned a lesson. To this day, I have a great deal of cautious respect for bulls, no matter how gentle they may seem. I have never forgotten that day in my very young life when I came face to face with a lot-a-bull.

Uncle Bill, the Barber

"Time for hair cuts!" Ma announced. That sent my brother and me scurrying from the room. We knew we wouldn't win the game of hide-and-seek with Ma. But we wanted to make a point: We hated it!

Ma always cut our hair. She had a scissors that she used for cutting material, paper, cardboard, and whatever else a scissors was needed for around the house. Needless to say, it was not very sharp since it was used for everything imaginable. Nevertheless, with this scissors and a comb, Ma cut our hair.

One day when Ma came home from town, she teasingly said to my brother and me, "I have something special for you." My brother and I began jumping up and down wondering what the surprise might be. She explained that she had stopped to see her uncle, Bill the barber. She told us all about her conversation with good ol' Uncle Bill. She told us that she had asked if he might have a used clipper that she could buy.

Uncle Bill was a kind-hearted soul. "Just a minute," he responded. "Let me look around a bit."

After some time in the back room, Uncle Bill emerged. "Look what I found," he gleefully announced. He explained, "I know that you folks don't have electricity so I found just the thing for you."

"Look," Ma said as she held it out proudly. "Uncle Bill said he couldn't use it anymore and didn't want it, so he gave it to us." We were a bit skeptical about it all, but Ma was so happy that we quietly played along. However, we soon found out why Uncle Bill didn't want it anymore!

I was the first one in the family to experience haircutting with this non-electric, hand-operated clipper. It had two handles. As they were squeezed together, the little blades crossed each other and cut hair. At least, that is what they were supposed to do. But this clipper had cut a great deal of hair and was very dull.

"Ouch! That hurt!" The clipper mostly "pulled" rather than clipped. When I moved my head in response, it "pulled" even more.

But Ma would just say, "Sorry," and continue on. It was torture! But Ma insisted upon using the clipper instead of going back to the scissors and comb method. "After all, it is a step up," she laughingly quipped. Indeed, who would want to get in the way of progress? And besides, "It does a much nicer job," Ma continued to remind us.

Then one day, when I was about to take my place in the "torture chair" to get my hair pulled out, Ma told me that the clipper was broken. "Yippee!" I shouted.

"But," she added, "we'll take it to Uncle Bill. He can fix it for us." So, the next time we went to town we stopped at Uncle Bill's barber shop.

"Sure," Uncle Bill agreed, "I'll take a look at it in a minute." In a short time, he had a break from customers. He took the clipper and headed toward the back room.

"I'm sorry to bother you further," Ma apologetically called after her uncle, "But is it possible to sharpen it?"

"Of course," Uncle Bill responded, "I should have thought of that before. I'll be back in a bit."

Sharpening it! What a novel idea. Now that could really help. For sure, it couldn't possibly make it worse, I thought to myself.

In about 15 minutes, Uncle Bill was back. He handed the clipper to Ma. "As good as new," he said with a smile. Before Ma could respond, he looked down at me. Putting his hand on my head he observed, "I think this young lad needs a haircut. Why don't we do that right now?" And before anyone could respond, he grabbed me and heisted me up into that big barber chair. What a big chair! "Well," Uncle Bill observed, "just a minute." He picked up a padded board and put it across the arms behind me. "Alright, young man," he commented, "Let me lift you up to the next level."

So far this was all kind of fun. But then, "Oh no, another large white sheet. Just like tonsil surgery," I muttered. Uncle Bill paid no attention. He draped the white sheet over me and fastened it tightly around my neck.

I closed my eyes, clenched my teeth together, and gripped the arms of the chair as tightly as I could. At first, Uncle Bill clipped with a comb and a very sharp scissors. That didn't hurt at all. Was that all there was to it? Soon that question was answered. Uncle Bill put down the comb and scissors and picked up another tool. He politely explained to me, "This is an electric clipper." I was afraid. If Ma's clipper hurts, this electric one must really hurt! I took a fresh grip on the arms of the chair, expecting the worst. Suddenly, I heard a gentle humming sound. I felt this nice warm buzzing on my neck. And it didn't hurt at all! I could hardly believe it. Oh, if only Uncle Bill could cut my hair every time. But that was not possible. After all, it cost fifty cents! That would almost buy a sack of groceries.

Ma's clipper worked a little better. But it was still a painful experience. So each time it was my turn to get into the infamous chair, I braced myself tensely waiting for the next pull of the clipper. I was always so thankful each time when Ma finally announced, "Ok, I'm done." Another grueling session in the torture chair was over!

A Sad Day–
A Happy Day

How far back in our young lives do we remember incidences or happenings? Most of my remembrances begin when I was about 5 years old. However, there is one occurrence that indelibly sticks in my memory from when I was between two and three years old. It was the saddest day of my young life. My oldest sister, Leone, who was twelve years older than I, was like my second mother. From little on, she carried me around, fed me, and rocked me to sleep. But then one day she was telling me that she would not be at home as much anymore. She had been offered a job as a nanny for a family in town. She was in high school and had an opportunity to earn her room and board plus a small salary. Since our house was very small, it seemed good to take advantage of this offer. Besides, she would be paid thirty-five cents a day!

Probably one of the most difficult tasks for her was to break the news to me, her little brother. She and I had grown very close and she had spoiled me as much as possible. One day she took me on her knee and was taking great pains to break the news to me gently. She explained, "I will not be here as much anymore to hold you and fix your 'owies' and rock you to sleep. I will be staying with some nice people in town, working for them and going to school. So I want you to be a good boy, listen to Ma and do what she wants you to do."

As I sat on her lap, listening intently, I sensed that this was a rather difficult time for both of us. When she was all finished with her simple and carefully worded explanation, I looked at her with a tear trickling down my cheek and summed it all up in my best vocabulary, "Eo byo bebye moi moi?" (Translation: "Leone will rock-abye Levi no more?") Well, soon we were both crying and hugging as though we would never see each other again. But, of course, we would. Yet, through the years, I have never forgotten that tender moment.

(Siblings can be such a wonderful blessing to each other when they are young and when they grow older. I never had the privilege of having either of my sisters in my life in their later years. Leone, who was practically my second mother, was taken to her heavenly home when she was but 42 years old. My other sister, Viola, was received by her Lord when she was but 21 years of age. Praise the Lord for those wonderful years of blessing that we had together.)

A few years later, I was old enough for school. Leone, desperately, wanted to become a teacher. I was her captive pupil. She, very patiently, taught me to count, to recite the alphabet, and other basics. But before I went to school, she seemed insistent upon teaching me my opening statement to my teacher.

She didn't care much for my first name, Levi. You see, I was supposed to be a girl. Ma told me later that she had already chosen my name. It was Mary! What a nice name. But it didn't seem appropriate for a boy. So how was it that I was named Levi? Ma told me.

"So why not use my name?" Pa suggested, "Why not?" He insisted.

"But then he went too far," Ma recalled.

"Why not a pure junior, Levi Eli Redlin II?"

That is when Ma, a very soft-spoken and gentle woman, said that she put her foot down and insisted, "Absolutely not. Not another Levi Eli! One is plenty."

Well, negotiations began, and someone came up with the name Dale. "Well, it is better than Eli," someone suggested. Another quipped, "It is certainly better than Mary," since I was a boy. And so it was decided. Levi Dale it would be. But Ma and my siblings preferred Dale.

Now I was about to make my debut into the scariest place in the world: school. It was scary because we had little opportunity to play with other children. Our social life was pretty much, occasionally, going to town with Ma and Pa, attending church and Sunday school, and playing with my cousins a few times a year. So the social adjustment of attending school and mingling with children that we didn't know was difficult for all of us.

Leone was diligently coaching me in preparation for my first day of school. She was insistent that I make an impressive opening statement. Over and over again, she coached my recitation, "My name is Levi Dale Redlin, but I go by the name of Dale." I was ready!

What a nice teacher. Miss Munson greeted me at the door of the room where I would begin first grade. As I recall, my opening statement was a winner.

"I am Miss Munson, and what is your name?" the kind teacher inquired, giving me the perfect cue.

I pulled together all the courage and confidence I had and recited clearly, "My name is Levi Dale Redlin, but I go by the name of Dale."

"Well, how nice," Miss Munson responded. "I will try to remember that." My first day was a success, and I could go home and report that my recitation went just fine, much to the praise of my sister-coach and to the disappointment of Pa.

What are Galoshes?

We lived about one mile from town, so most of the children in school were "townies." Apparently their fathers had jobs of some sort, because most of them wore nice clothing bought from a store. What I noticed mostly, was that many of them had bicycles. They were nice, but I didn't dare think about the possibility of having one. It was just not possible. I knew that, and it didn't really bother me. I just admired them and watched the other children riding them and let it go at that. Our one possibility to have a bicycle lay buried in the ol' sand pit. But it was not yielding enough spare bike parts to build one. Nevertheless, we never stopped looking.

However, there was one thing that I wished for. I hoped that some day, somehow, I could get a pair of boys' overshoes. We usually wore hand-me-downs. But for some reason no hand-me-down boys' overshoes ever came our way. Yet, we did have some old girls' overshoes. Mom was good at making things over into something else. She could turn an old girl's blouse or a flour sack into a little boy's shirt. But she really couldn't do anything to make over girls' overshoes. So on winter days when the snow was deep, Ma found some old overshoes. Often times, they were my sister's with the extended heel. She pulled them on my little feet and snapped them so they wouldn't fall off. They always felt squishy when I walked because of the extended heel.

I was not ashamed to wear shirts made out of flour sacks, or pants that were six inches too short, or carry a syrup bucket for my lunch, but wearing girls' overshoes was a bit much for me. Yet, I knew that there was nothing else. So when Pa took us to school, whether it was with the sleigh or car, I begged him to drop us off a short distance from the school. I lingered within hearing-distance waiting for the bell to ring. Then I allowed some time for the children to go inside. When I thought the other children were out of the way and the "coast was clear," I carefully entered the front door and rushed into the coat room, hoping to be the last one in. It was better to be late than to chance someone seeing my overshoes! Even before I hung up my winter coat, scarf, and cap, I removed my overshoes and hid them behind the door, hoping no one would find them.

Recess was often a tricky time because Miss Munson wanted everyone to go outside. If it was overshoe day, I usually said I had to go to the bathroom and then sort of lingered, taking my time, and getting back just before class time. After all, it was such a nice bathroom. It was all clean. It had sinks with hot and cold running water as well as paper towels. There were toilets that flushed, not to mention the neat rolls of toilet paper. I was accustomed to an outdoor toilet stocked with pages from the Sears Roebuck catalog. What a difference! Indeed, it was a pleasant experience to be there, even though I would have much preferred going outside to play.

Our teacher was very helpful. When school was out, she helped the children get their winter clothes on and made certain that they had found all of their wraps, as she called them. When it was overshoe day, I was never in a hurry. I stalled, waiting for all of them to finish and hustle out for their ride or walk the few blocks to their home in town. Well, at least, I had to begin dressing. I suppose Miss Munson thought I was the pokiest child she had ever seen.

One day, Miss Munson was being just too helpful. She was still there and all the children had left. Now what do I do? I was all dressed except for my overshoes. She looked me over and said kindly, "Now Dale, let me help you. Where are your galoshes?"

I had no idea what she was talking about. I had never heard that word before. I very honestly looked up at her and said, "I don't have any, Miss Munson."

"Oh," she said, "You really need to get some."

I answered softly, "Okay."

Finally, she left. I pulled the door back, retrieved my girls' overshoes and scampered down the hall holding them closely to my body hoping no one could see them. I kept on going down the steps and into the snow until I was a safe distance from school. Then I put them on over my snowy, wet feet and headed for home.

We usually walked home. It was only a mile. I always had plenty of time on the way to think and wonder and dream. *Galoshes. What are they?* I wondered. *What are they used for? Maybe I will ask Ma when I get home.* But when I got home, it didn't seem important anymore. At home I was in another world, the one where I felt comfortable, happy, and could just be me without being concerned about fitting in. Anyway, I had to get to the battery-operated radio to listen to my favorite program, "Jack Armstrong, The All-American Boy."

"I bet Jack never had to wear girls' overshoes," I muttered to myself.

The Run-Away Bike–
The Run-Away Pony

What a surprise when one day Pa brought home a pony. One of Pa's friends was moving and had no place to keep the pony for a few weeks. I was quite small, so he seemed like a big pony to me. They called it a Shetland pony.

He was mostly brown with a black mane and tail. I thought he was pretty, but I didn't want to ride him. My older brothers and sisters had much fun with this unexpected pet. Besides, when their friends from town heard about the pony, they came out in droves most every Saturday to ride it. There were more friends than my siblings ever knew they had. But my brothers and sisters liked that because they came out on their bicycles. The friends tried to ride the pony and my brothers and sisters tried to ride the bicycles. I had such a good time watching the spills and thrills and the laughing that accompanied all of the fun.

I'll never forget the day one of my brothers, Charlie, mounted one of the older bikes. It was really in bad shape. The fenders were off. The paint was scratched and worn. It was dirty and the springs in the seat were hanging loose. Charlie climbed on this well-worn bike and made a few turns around the yard. Then he decided to head down the rather steep decline leading toward the barn. The bike picked up speed. It was going faster and faster. It looked like fun. But Charlie was heading straight for the barn! He was riding a run-away-bike that was totally out of control! Why didn't he try to stop?

Surprise, surprise—the brakes didn't work! Obviously, he was afraid to turn sharply to the left as the teen age "pros" knew how to do very well, especial-

ly when their brakes weren't working. The barn was getting ever closer and closer. Both of his feet were off the pedals, dangling in mid-air, as he plunged head-long toward the barn. Everyone stopped what they were doing and watched the run-away bicycle with my brother on board. What was going to happen? We soon found out as the bike slammed into the side of the barn with a thud! The bike lay on its side with the rear wheel spinning and my brother lay groaning on his back with a bruised and bloody forehead.

Charlie's head was badly bruised, but his pride was hurt even more. The bike needed even more repair than it needed before. They were talking about the forks and the front wheel being bent and that it couldn't be ridden anymore. Did this episode interrupt the fun of the day or stop the town friends from coming out to ride the pony? Not at all! The bike was thrown into the ol' sand pit and replaced with another one and they kept coming. Only, from that time on, whenever my brother straddled a bike, especially a newer one, someone would cry out teasingly, "Charlie, look out for the barn!"

I was this little five-year-old boy watching, laughing, and jumping up and down. I suppose I was just too obvious. In the midst of all the fun a couple of the boys grabbed me and started tossing me around in fun. Suddenly they stopped and looked at each other. One said, "Let's do it." I thought to myself, *do what?* I soon found out as they grabbed me and plopped me down on the pony's back. They put the reins in my hand and gave him a healthy slap on the rump. Off we went! As soon as the pony discovered that the rider was doing nothing to control him, he decided to go where he wanted to go. Where he wanted to go was easy for him to decide. There was a patch of lush green grass behind the house where our outhouse had been. The pony loved to go there to graze. So, off we went toward the "salad bar."

Besides me trying to hang on, there was another problem. I didn't think of it at the time as I was so busy trying to stay in the middle of his back. My legs were too short to hug his body, so I was like a ball bouncing

this way and then that. I dropped the reins and was tugging on his mane for dear life. Uh-oh, the clothes line. It was strung across the yard and just happened to be between the pony and his favorite lunch. It was not a problem for the pony because he fit under it rather easily. He had been there before!

The townies were laughing and cheering and yelling, "Hang on—hang on!"

Someone was screaming, "Look out for the clothes line!" Sorry, too late. There was nothing I could do. Like a shot, under the clothesline we went. The wire line caught me under the chin, whipped against my neck, and swept me cleanly from the back of the pony. I landed on the ground hardly able to breathe. As the pony pushed his nose deeply into the lush grass, my "friends" carried me into the house. As I was croaking and trying to breathe, Ma was examining the purple mark across my neck. Though she was very upset with what happened, she felt confident that eventually my voice would return to normal and that apparently no serious injury had resulted. It took some time, but eventually my throat healed and the hoarseness left.

It is said that if one falls off a horse, one should get right back on and ride again. I never did that. In fact, I never rode the pony again. A few weeks later, Pa's friend picked up the pony. I had no regrets, but the "townies" most certainly did.

A Dream Came True

It was a beautiful, early fall day and we were about to take a trip. Normally, we never went far from home. It was the high point in the week if we were invited to go along to town when Pa took Ma in to do her "trading." That's what many called it; not "shopping" but "trading." That was because many farmers took with them a can of cream and a few dozen eggs to trade for groceries. Sometimes, Ma could spare a nickel each for my brother and me. We usually traded this for a big, double-dipped ice cream cone at Fairmont's ice cream store. That was my kind of "trade!"

Our other trips were to visit relatives. The longest trip we ever took was to visit Pa's brother, who lived almost 30 miles from our place. That was a long way! But the trip that we were about to take was even longer. It was all the way to Aberdeen, South Dakota. That was 100 miles away! I thought to myself, *That will take all day!* As it turned out, it did!

The reason for the trip? Well, my oldest sister, Leone, had graduated from high school. That was a special milestone of sorts in our family. My oldest brother had started high school but then quit to help on the farm. Ma had graduated from the eighth grade and Pa got as far as the third grade. So my oldest sister had broken through the family tradition barrier, so to speak. But her ambitions were not satisfied. For many years she had talked of becoming a teacher. Fortunately, her minor experiences in trying to prepare me for first grade had not discouraged her.

Going to college didn't seem possible because it was terribly expensive. Yet, she did not give up on her dream. After high school, she and my oldest brother, Royal, rented an apartment in town. Leone worked at various jobs and Royal set pins at Tommy's Bowling Alley (this was done by hand before pin setting machines).

Leone was able to save some money, but at a quarter an hour, she was still very short of the necessary funds for college. Nevertheless, she contacted Northern State Teachers College at Aberdeen. "I would like to become a grade school teacher," she wrote, "however, I have very little money. Is it possible for me to work at the school during the year to help pay my tuition and room and board?" This was not an uncommon request. Many prospective students had the same problem then, as well as now.

The college administration answered. They encouraged my sister to enroll in the teacher training program. However, they also pointed out that most of the jobs at the school were already taken. Nevertheless, if she could come early she would be able to help clean and paint some of the dormitory rooms. This paid thirty cents an hour and would be applied to her bill at the college. She was ecstatic with the news. Plans were made and a trip to Aberdeen was scheduled. "The trip" was on!

Our car was not dependable, but Royal had saved enough from his job as pin-setter to buy a car. It was much newer than ours, but the tires were badly worn. Nevertheless, he offered to take it on the trip. We really didn't have another option. We all put on our "Sunday clothes." My sister gathered up the items that she had sewn as well as the warmer clothing she needed for winter. After all, since she was going 100 miles away, she might not get home for the entire year.

Pa observed, "We need to take along a tire pump, patching, and boots for the tires. They look a little thin."

In defense, my brother answered, "But I do have a spare tire."

Pa simply replied, "I know, I've seen it. I'll take along some extra patching." And so we were off on the longest trip many of us had ever taken.

The car was full. My sister had a friend who also had the desire to become a teacher so she was invited to come along. Why not? We had only eight travelers. Why not another? All totaled, there were nine of us plus the "luggage" of the two hopeful teachers. We were packed, literally packed, into Royal's two-door, 1934 Ford. The person in the passenger seat was loaded under with bags of clothes. My brother Eldon and I were half-standing, half-kneeling on the back floor board. Ma's lunch box was on the floor between us with a bag of clothing on top of it. Seat belts? Not a chance. Anyway, it was many decades before they were invented. Finally, we were off!

Everyone was in good spirits, laughing and kidding each other. Especially happy were the two students who were about to enter their "field of dreams."

The laughing and kidding came to an abrupt end, however, when, "BANG!" The car began to shake and rumble. My brother held the steering wheel tightly and guided his car off to the side of the road.

"What happened?" I asked, from my little compartment in the back.

My brother calmly assessed the situation in two simple words, "Flat tire." We piled out of the car and sure enough, there it was. A front tire had a huge hole in it. A blow out!

The men went to work. They tried to work carefully. After all, each was wearing his best pants and shirt. The blow out was too large to fix with a boot, so they had to use the tread-barren spare tire. The men jacked the car up, and in a rather short time the exchange was made. We squeezed back into our allotted space and were on our way. No one said anything, but everyone knew that now we were down to only four rather poor tires for the remainder of the trip.

It wasn't long before someone said something about eating. We had only thirty miles left to go so everyone agreed that we could stop to eat. Besides, we spotted a road-side area with grass and park benches. Ideal for a picnic and for stretching our limbs. "We've been making good time," my brother proudly commented as we maneuvered our way in turn out of the car.

We enjoyed a wonderful picnic. Pa stretched out on the grass and seemed to forget that we had a-ways to go. Also, we had to get my sister and friend into a dormitory room and try to return home before dark. The tires...remember? (See photo on Dedication Page)

We had gone only about five miles after lunch when..."Not again," everyone yelled in unison as that unmistakable rumbling noise told us that another tire had gone flat. Off to the side of the road we went again. The good news was that it hadn't blown out.

The bad news was that this would take longer than the blow out. The tire had to be removed and the tube patched. While my brother jacked up the car Pa got the tire patching and pump out. He had also brought along "tire removing wrenches." These were leaves from an old leaf spring. They worked great to pry the tire off the rim in order to get at the tube to patch it. It went well but took quite some time.

As we finally turned into the campus of the college, I was so happy I could be along. I couldn't imagine anyone going this far away from home for school! Yet, I was very proud as my sister and her friend walked up the steps to get their assigned dormitory room. I wondered, *Will I ever be doing this?* She would be here for three quarters or nine months. Upon graduation she would be prepared to teach grades 1–8.

Her room, one she would share with three other girls, was rather small. No matter—she was used to that. The dormitory needed cleaning but it was very nice. It had indoor plumbing! In the bathroom was a large shower room. *That sure has the one beat at home that Charlie tried to build,* I thought to myself. He made that out of an old out house with a barrel mounted on top. It didn't work very well. Especially not when someone replaced the sun-warmed water with cold well water!

In the next room were many sinks and stools. The water from the faucets ran hot or cold water! There was a nice laundry room with some electric washing machines, irons, and ironing boards. Ma's eyes lit up, and by the look of her smile, I wondered if maybe she wanted to enroll in college too—just so she could use the bathroom and laundry.

All of the passengers stayed in the waiting room as Pa and Ma, with the two prospective students, went into an office at the administration building. They had to make arrangements for paying the college tuition and book fees as well as the room and board. I wondered how they were ever going to pay for that. I found out later that it would cost a total of $250 for the school year. There was $70 for tuition, $11 for fees, $34 for room and $135 for board. I couldn't comprehend how it could cost so much!

Finally, we said our good-byes. It felt rather strange as we seven got back into the car. More room, no bags of clothes, no lunch, smooth tires—and 100 miles to go! I, actually, got to sit on part of the back seat on the way home. We had only one more flat tire on the way home, which they had to fix in the dark. I slept through it all. Finally, we drove into the driveway. My brother was proud that he had driven all the way himself. We were all tired. Some talked of something to eat but I went straight to bed. I could hear Pa and Ma talking for quite some time. In the morning I found out what they had been talking about. It was not good. My favorite cow, Bessie, had to be sold!

Selling Bessie

It was Friday. When I awoke, Pa and Ma had been up for some time. The chores were done and breakfast was ready. We ate in silence. I knew something was bothering Pa and Ma.

Finally, Pa said to me, "How about going to the sale barn with me today?" Friday was sale day. The sale barn was located a rather short distance from our home. Sometimes we walked across the field to a sale just for something to do. Pa visited with people he knew. I always enjoyed listening to the auctioneer. Nick was my favorite and the favorite of many. Sometimes he stopped in the middle of his auctioneering chant and told a joke or made a funny comment about something that was happening. As a result, others, as well as we, came to the auction barn just to visit and listen to Nick the auctioneer. Nick affectionately referred to such people as "sale flies." They came just for the fun of it and hardly ever bought a thing.

So, when Pa invited me to go along with him to the auction barn, it was not unusual. As we were about to walk out of the house, however, something rather different happened. Pa and Ma hugged and Pa assured Ma, "It's going to be okay. We'll get along."

I was trying to understand what Pa and Ma were concerned about. I would find out soon enough. We walked to the barn. Pa opened the door and took a halter from the wall and put it on Bessie, one of our three milk cows. She was such a nice cow. She didn't produce as much milk as each of the other two but her milk was very rich. We got lots of cream from her to use for making butter as well as Ma's baking. Besides, Bessie really helped fill the cream can to take to town for trading.

"Where are we taking Bessie?" I questioned.

"Well," Pa answered, "It costs money to go to college. I don't know how much money Bessie will bring. But it's all we can do."

"You're going to sell Bessie?" I blurted out with alarm. "How can we do that? She gives us a calf every year and we sell cream from her every week for groceries. And—and—she's such a nice cow." Pa didn't answer. He opened the stanchion and Bessie dutifully pulled her head out as Pa guided her toward the door.

"Sometimes," Pa began to say rather haltingly, "Sometimes we have to do things we don't want to do in order to do what is right." With that, Pa led Bessie out of the barn door.

Across the pasture and through the gate we walked, slowly, silently, sadly. I didn't say anything because I knew if I tried to talk I would start to cry. But I wanted to go along. Bessie was my favorite. When she spotted any of us in the pasture she always walked over to us. She liked to have her head scratched and patted. She never got enough of it. I knew we were doing this to help pay for my sister's education. That helped a little. But still, I wondered, why? Since we are doing the right thing for the right reason, why does it hurt so much? Why does it make me so sad?

Pa checked Bessie in at the sales office. Then we went into the bleachers surrounding the sales ring to watch. It wasn't the same as before. So many times we had come to the sales barn and I had always enjoyed it. But this time I didn't want to be there; but yet I did.

Many cattle were being herded through the gate into the sales ring, from one to ten at a time. Nick, the auctioneer, was in good voice, selling the livestock coming through the ring and joking with the people. I wasn't laughing.

Finally, the gate opened and Bessie came through it. She looked bewildered and scared. Men were yelling and cracking whips. I had not seen this in the same way ever before! Nick, the auctioneer, began, "$25 biddin' now $30, 30, would ya make it 30—give me 30, bid-di-bum-da $30, would give me $30, whodada bid a $30 bid... ?"

"Thirty dollars is a lot of money," I thought, *"But is that enough for Bessie?"* I wanted to bid but I didn't have any money and I knew that they wouldn't take my bid anyway.

Suddenly, Nick stopped his chant. I wondered, *What now?* Nick asked, "Alright, whose cow is this?" Pa raised his arm. Nick recognized Pa immediately. "Oh, it's you Levi. Would you tell us about this cow?" Everyone was silent as Pa answered with a glowing report of dear ol' Bessie. Then Nick looked straight at me. "And how about you, young man? Can you tell us anything about her?" I wanted to disappear under the bleachers but I needed to say something for Bessie. Nick urged, "Well, you better say what you want to say, now. This is your last chance."

As I started to speak, I just couldn't help it. Tears started to roll down my checks and all I could say was, "She's really a nice cow and her name is Bessie."

The crowd chuckled as Nick turned his attention back, "Alright then, where were we? For one thing, that's not enough money for this good milk cow. You heard from the boy. Now let's get at it." Nick started his chant and soon the bids were coming in right and left. Finally, Nick hit the gavel on the desk, "Sold!" he said firmly, "For $56.00. Not enough!"

I sat with a lump in my stomach. I asked Pa if we could leave. He said we could.

As we walked out of the sales ring, I asked if we could go out into the pens and see Bessie one last time. Pa agreed. After searching the many pens, we finally found her. She came over to the gate and I scratched her head and patted her one last time.

As we were about to leave, a rather young man came and stopped beside us. "Was this your cow?" he asked. Pa answered that it was. "Well," he said, "I just want you to know that I am the one who bought her. We really need a cow since we have none. I have been looking for one to furnish milk, cream, and butter for my family." There was silence. Then he looked at me and continued, "I understand her name is Bessie. My children will be glad to hear that she has a name. Well, I just want you to know that she will have a good home and a family who will take good care of her and love her."

Pa looked at me and I at him with a little bit of a smile. Then we both responded at the same time, "Thank you." Pa continued, "We feel much better now. Enjoy Bessie."

We walked home with lighter hearts knowing that we did the right thing and Bessie would be loved and cared for. And besides, I really learned a lot about making difficult decisions and doing what is right, even though sometimes it hurts a lot.

My sister, Leone, graduated and taught in the country schools for a number of years. In fact, she was my teacher when I was in the seventh and eighth grades. After marrying, she returned to college and earned her Bachelor of Science degree from Northern State Teacher's College in elementary education.

The Last of August–
Melons on the Move

Our neighbor, August, was at the end of his rope. Not literally, thankfully, but financially. He had no money and the yearly payment on his farm was due on the first of March. August had not been able to make his farm payments for 3 years. Finally, the bank that held the mortgage foreclosed. August had to move.

August was a good-natured fellow. He always looked on the bright side of things. His cup was always half full, never half empty. Besides, he knew that many of his friends and neighbors were experiencing similar problems. August decided to advertise his plight without shame and with a little bit of humor. He scratched together enough money for a gallon of paint. Since his farm payment was due on the first of March, across the front of his barn for all to see, he painted these words: "THE FIRST OF MARCH IS THE LAST OF AUGUST."

It wasn't really a laughing matter, but Pa laughed and laughed. He knew August and his sense of humor. It seemed that the general attitude was that since one could do nothing about it, one may as well have a good laugh, at least.

Because of the extended drought and the economic depression of the 30's, many farm families were hardly able to meet their basic family needs with nothing available to meet the payments on their farms. As a result, many farms were repossessed by financial institutions. As the crops were practically nonexistent and the depression in the economy continued, the banks became owners of much property. Attempting to manage these farms while realizing little or no profit proved to be a genuine financial "headache" for the

banks. They practically begged farmers to try to buy them. As a result, Pa bought many farms during that time. Time and again he made the payment of a few dollars down with the promise to make payments if the crops grew. They didn't. We moved. We fully understood what August was going through.

Pa's friend, Joe, marveled at Pa's never-give-up attitude. Joe preferred to play it safe and rent his little farm with no intention of ever buying it. He simply observed as Pa continually tried to buy farm after farm. One day, as he was visiting at our place and exchanging stories with Pa, he summed it all up rather accurately,

"Ya know Levi," he blurted out in his coarse, raspy voice, "If ya had all the land ya ever bought, ya'd really have a heck of a lot of land."

A final blow was struck, however, when Pa and Ma lost their small savings. They had tried to put aside a small amount to use for some future opportunity that might present itself. They had deposited it in a "safe" place, a bank; the bank where Pa's brother worked. But then came the financial crash of the thirties! Banks went broke—utterly broke. They closed their doors. There was no such thing as the FDIC. Depositors were simply left with nothing. So Pa's dreams of owning a farm were put on hold. He had reluctantly, temporarily assumed Joe's attitude and rented a small, rural place a short distance from town. There, Pa tried to find ways to make a few dollars for our livelihood.

One idea that I will never forget was our attempt to raise melons. Out in the barnyard there was an old straw-pile bottom. Years before, someone had threshed grain there and blew the straw on a pile. It had decayed, with time, leaving a rich patch of humus. Pa surmised that this could be a good place to grow melons. We managed to get seed for a few types of melons and in the spring we seeded our melon patch. We had a good water well, so moisture was not a problem. How did we transport the buckets of water to the melon patch? Of course, with my little ol' rusty, wobbly wagon.

What a crop of melons! We had watermelons and muskmelons galore. I was hauling water and generously keeping the plot wet. Finally, Pa warned me, "Now, don't water them too much. That will not be good for them." That never dawned on me. I thought, *more water, bigger melons!*

Finally, they were ready to pick and sell. How should we do that? Well, Pa thought we should try something we hadn't tried before. "Let's load up the grain wagon with melons and go to town. We should be able to sell a few, at least. "

We had more than we thought. The grain wagon box was almost full! Into town we went and down the street we came. Pa found a corner where we could park, not far from the main grocery store. He had made a sign: FRESH MELONS—One-5 cents. Three-10 cents.

It wasn't very long before we had a good trade going. We were selling melons as fast as we could get them to the customers. It was fun! Pa was smiling from ear to ear. When someone tapped Pa on his back, Pa turned to help whom he thought was a customer. Surprise, surprise! Pa discovered it was a policeman with a billy club in his hand. Pa recognized him immediately.

"Hello, Frank," Pa greeted, "how many melons do you want?"

Frank smiled sheepishly and began to explain. "See, Levi, here's the thing. What you are doing is against the law. I presume you don't have a peddler's permit."

Pa answered openly, "You're right Frank. All I've got is a load of melons. And you know what, Frank? They're selling like hot cakes."

"I know, I know," responded Frank. "And they do look mighty good."

"Here," Pa picked up a couple of choice melons. "Take these home for your family."

"Don't do that!" Frank responded. "You are making this more difficult. I'll tell you what to do, Levi. Now listen carefully. When I leave, you must move. But just

67

go to a different corner. As I make my rounds it will take some time to get back to this area. If you haven't sold them all when you see me coming, you will need to move again. By the time you have moved a couple of times, you should be rid of your melons."

Pa graciously answered, "Thank you, Frank."

But Pa couldn't let it go. He had to say one last time, "But Frank, are you sure you don't want any melons?" Frank just shook his head and walked away. Frank was right. After a couple moves we were rid of the melons! If I remember correctly, it seems that Pa had something over $10.00. That would buy quite a few sacks of groceries!

People were usually quite considerate of each other. Frank knew that Pa was simply trying to make a few dollars to feed his family. Besides, it was just a short-term operation, so Frank chose to "look the other way."

Pa never gave up trying to find work wherever he could. Finally, he became involved in a government program called the WPA, Works Progress Administration. This and a number of other government sponsored programs were often referred to simply as "Relief." And that they were. They were a relief from much of the stress and hardship felt by many during those years.

For some time, Pa, with his team of horses, went to work for the WPA every day to help build roads. Whenever I drive highway 212 west of Watertown, I still think about how hard Pa and others worked with horses, one-bottom plows, hand-held dirt scrapers, shovels, and pick-axes to build at least part of that highway. Whenever I visit State Parks, I see the fingerprints of the WPA everywhere. Buildings, trails, and stone work carry the signature of the many skilled as well as unskilled workers on those crews. They knew how to put in a day's work and welcomed the chance to do so for a very small wage.

Movin' Again

In 1939, Pa was ready to buy another farm. Ma had inherited a little money when her father, my grandfather, died. After paying off debts, she had $350.00 left. Pa wanted to use this money for a down payment on yet another farm. Ma had been through this so many times. She didn't want to discuss it. But Pa was very enthused and also quite persuasive. "This is the best deal we have ever been offered. Things have to get better soon. Besides, we are almost fifty years old. It's either now or never. Besides that," Pa pointed out, "With Royal (my oldest brother) getting married, they need a place to live. They can move into this place and we will, finally, have a farm of our own." Well, after a great deal of discussion and Pa's relentless persuasiveness, Ma reluctantly agreed.

The "deal" was this: the bank agreed to sell us this 300 acre farm, with buildings (sort of), for $300.00 down and $300.00 each year until it was paid for. The total price was $6000.00. We didn't want to think of the total price because that was an unbelievable amount of money at the time. (In today's money that might be approximately $150,000.) But maybe, just maybe, the crops would finally grow and we might be able to harvest enough to make the payment.

There were lots of mights and maybes. It would be a struggle. The land had not been farmed properly for many years. Evidence of weeds, that seemed to grow no matter how dry, was everywhere. Our machinery was old and horse drawn. We had no money and only a few head of livestock. But we had each other and, most of all, we had God. With the Lord's blessing we were convinced that there would be a way to meet our commitments. The trials and hardships that we experienced drew us close together and strengthened us in our faith. We were a happy family. Though we had hardly anything as far as this world's possessions, we were never depressed. With the Lord in our lives and the stability of our parents, life was good!

Moving day was exciting for us children. We were moving about ten miles. Pa had to make at least three or four trips with the horses and hay wagon, our "moving van." We kids found somewhere to ride amidst the furniture, tools, and equipment. Pa pulled the machinery over later with the horses, one piece at a time.

Pa was very excited. He said time and again, "This is the best farm we have ever tried to buy." Not that the buildings were well kept. But there were buildings! Not that the land was in such great shape, but with much work and the Lord's blessing we all expected good things to happen.

Rodents and insects of all kinds had pretty much taken over the living quarters and set up "housekeeping." Here and there the plaster had fallen from the ceiling and walls. Major cleaning would be the order of the day for some time in this old, two-story farm house. We started with the shovel and finally got to the broom and the scrub-brush stage.

The creaky door that opened to the basement especially intrigued us kids. Whenever the front door opened or closed, the basement door swung loosely back and forth, creaking like doors we had heard on the spooky radio shows.

I wanted to go down the narrow steps that led to the basement, but I wouldn't go without someone. Finally, Pa relented, lit a kerosene lantern, and we slowly made our way down into the dark, moist, and windowless basement. The steps were varied in spacing. Some were loose, some were broken.

As we carefully made our way, we heard all kinds of scratching, scraping, and squeaking sounds. I asked Pa what it was. He replied that it must be mice. He was right. But not only mice! As Pa held the lantern up, we saw there were bugs, spiders, and mice, as well as rats and salamanders, everywhere. They must have been surprised. After all, this had been their own private den for a long time. There was a lot of activity as they all seemed to try to find a hole or crevice to hide in. There were plenty of those!

The salamanders weren't quite so fast. We could feel a few of them getting squished under our feet as we cautiously took a few steps. We peered into the dim shadows, and there, staring back at us, were sharp, piercing eyes reflecting the light of the lantern. From the walls and ledges and holes came the silent challenge of our right to invade their private domain.

It appeared that the windowless walls were mostly dirt, as was the floor. There was a wall on two sides of the basement made of field stone, with a little crumbling mortar here and there. It was very cool and damp with the smell of wet dirt and mold in the air. Spider webs hung everywhere as though guarding this haven for wildlife.

"Well," Pa said, "guess we've got a little work to do down here." Talk about the under-statement of the year. But years went by before we could afford to do much of anything to improve the basement. Eventually, one wall fell in and we were forced to make some repair. But it served as storage. We kept root crops in barrels of sand. Canning was stacked here and there. Ma set traps for the rodents but the population didn't seem to diminish.

Finally, we adopted Pa's surefire method of rodent control. We placed five-gallon buckets half-full of water here and there. The rats and mice trying to drink slipped and fell to a watery grave. What a job it was to carry the buckets with a load of dead rodents up the stairs to bury them outside. Joe was right. It was too much work! The salamanders continued, unharmed, in their dark, damp kingdom, much to Ma's dismay.

Chris the Painter

The first year went by quickly. Pa received a letter from the banker. He would be coming to see us and collect the $300.00 we owed. We didn't have 300 cents to spare, say nothing of $300.00. The crops had not been good. We had a few chickens, two pigs, a couple of milk cows and our team of horses. What little grain we were able to raise and the hay we were able to make was being used to feed the livestock.

What should we do? Pa and Ma, especially, had worked so very hard to clean things up. They really didn't want to move again. Pa had an idea. He knew that the bank didn't want the farm back. They had repossessed more property than they could handle as it was. Pa's thinking went like this: *Maybe, if we could do something clearly obvious to convince the banker that we were improving the buildings and the farm in general he would be convinced to give us another year's time.* Of course, we had done much, but a lot of it wasn't apparent to the casual observer. Pa said, "We have to do something that will impress the banker when he comes out. We have to do something that will catch his eye."

Pa ran his idea by Ma: "What do you think about painting the buildings?"

"What!" Ma responded in shock, "It seems to me that paint costs money. We barely have enough to buy groceries every week."

"Well, I know," Pa responded, "But maybe we can scrape enough together to get started, at least. The banker needs to be convinced that we are really trying."

As usual, Ma gave in and robbed the "cookie jar" of the egg money for the week's groceries and gave it to Pa.

Pa went to town. He came home with two five-gallon pails of paint, one white and one red. With a couple of old paint brushes that we had we went to work. The wood was very dry, as one might expect. It drank in the paint like a thirsty horse at the watering tank. Pa said, "As long as we have enough to paint the fronts of the house and the barn, it'll be just fine. That's the first thing that the banker will see as he comes up the driveway."

We began on the house. The immediate improvement was very striking. The little bit of paint that remained on the house was a dingy brown. The barn was mostly gray, weathered siding. Pa could hardly get any painting done. He kept walking out on the driveway to see how the appearance was improving. Finally, we used up all of the white paint and had finished painting one side and the front of the house. What a difference!

Now, the barn. We were about to start when we had a surprise visit. A man driving a rather dilapidated model A Ford pickup came up the driveway and into the yard. By the appearance of the vehicle, we were certain it was not the banker who sold us the farm. A rather small, mostly bald, middle-aged man jumped gingerly out of the pickup. He wore a pair of rather snug-fitting, tweed pants. His suspenders pulled his pants up much farther than necessary, exposing high-top shoes and argyle stockings.

We met him about halfway between the house and the barn. With his hand extended, he walked toward Pa and introduced himself, "I am Chris Quaman. I deal in antiques and collectables." He talked like he

walked, short and jerky. He chatted with Pa for awhile. Then he asked if he could use a small corner of our barn for storage. What was he planning to store? Some of his "antiques." As we soon discovered, the "antiques" were actually people's unwanted, badly used or worn-out items of junk, depending on one's point of view. But, of course, Pa couldn't say "no." So Chris cranked up the old Ford and jerked his way over to the barn to unload his valuable cargo.

Chris noticed that we were carrying paint brushes. "What ya paintin'?" Chris inquired in his sharp, rather high-pitched voice. Pa informed him that we were about to start painting the barn. "I can do that," Chris quickly answered. "I'm a painter." This, certainly, was no surprise. It appeared from his conversation that he claimed to be almost everything else! Why not a painter? Though Pa gently tried to dissuade him he would not hear of it. He promised that he would be out in the morning to help. But before he left, he made something very clear to Pa, "I will need the entire five-gallon pail of paint, because I paint with two brushes at a time!"

Pa looked at us with a twinkle in his eyes, and with a slight hesitation, Pa accepted Chris's offer. "We will be expecting you in the morning, Chris," Pa said in parting and with a wave of his hand.

78

In the morning, after chores and breakfast, we started to paint. But we couldn't help but glance down the road from time to time. We all wondered if Chris would really show up. We could hardly wait to see this proposed demonstration of human dexterity. We had never seen anybody try to paint with two paint brushes before and we doubted that it could be done without wasting much paint. We tried it. It didn't work.

Down the road Chris came, dust curling behind his rickety old pickup. His vehicle had barely stopped and Chris jumped out like a man on a mission. He came half-running toward the barn wearing the same tweed, high-water pants with suspenders and walking with his signature short, jerky steps. He carried a large paint brush in each hand. Pa went out to greet him but he was all business.

"Where's the paint?" Chris barked. Pa wasted no time getting the paint positioned for him. "Close to the barn," Chris ordered crisply as he adjusted the ladder.

We all stood and watched with anticipation. Finally, Chris was ready. He plunged the two brushes into the pail and began flailing away. Pa found a nice grassy spot on which to stretch out. Leaning on one elbow with a spear of grass in his mouth, Pa was ready for the show. After all, we didn't have much live entertainment in the area. This promised to be the best show we had seen for some time.

This jack-of-all-trades painted as though he were in a race. Up the ladder, down the ladder, filling the brushes, dripping on his clothes, his hands, his arms, and everywhere! Even his balding head was sprinkled with red paint. Paint was being wasted, but who could stop this comedy?

How long can this go on? We wondered.

Well, not long, as we expected. After about fifteen minutes, Chris suddenly remembered that he had some business to attend to in town. He cleaned his hands, head, face, and brushes with rags as well as possible. As he strutted toward his car, he looked back over his shoulder and promised, "I'll be back as soon as possible."

Pa thanked him and off Chris went like he was late for something. He never came back to help paint. We didn't mind that. We were trying to make the paint go as far as possible. The fun was over. We finished painting with one boring brush at a time!

The Banker Visits

Finally, we finished painting the immediately visible parts of both the house and barn. Not any too soon. After a few days, as we were tidying up the yard, a shiny, new, black car came heading down the road that passed by our place. This road was not heavily traveled, so when we noticed a car traveling in our direction, there was a good chance it would be turning into our driveway. Indeed, it did! Our banker friend had arrived. Pa and Ma politely invited him into the house but he declined. He preferred to simply talk things over with Pa in his nice shiny car. Pa later told us about their conversation, point by point.

After a little chit-chat, the well-dressed and congenial banker paused for a bit. Pa related to us, "I knew that the moment of truth had arrived."

"Well, Levi," the banker began. "You probably know why I am here. As we agreed, $300.00 is due to the bank in two weeks time."

Pa sat there with not three pennies in his pocket, no money in the bank, and hardly any livestock. So Pa explained, "We have tried hard to make some improvements and spent much time and labor in cleaning everything up. At the same time, we are beginning to get the land into tillable condition."

Undeniably, all of our work was very beneficial to the bank. The banker was impressed.

"Yes, Levi, I can see how much nicer everything looks. You have even painted the buildings," the banker volunteered. Then Pa told the banker what he dreaded to have to tell him.

Pa informed him, "We have spent any extra money on improvements, and now we simply don't have any money for the payment." The banker silently gazed out of the window seeming to carefully consider the things that Pa had said.

Finally, the banker inquired, "Could you pay us at least $100?"

Pa responded without hesitation, "I'm sorry. Perhaps we can pay more than one payment next year." Pa suggested, " But, as of now, we are simply unable to pay anything."

The banker was quiet for awhile. He looked out into the yard again, seeming to survey the looks of the property. Pa said his stomach was tied in knots. What might the banker say next? Would we have to move again after all of our hard work? Besides that, we liked this place. It was really beginning to feel like home.

Finally, the banker turned to Pa and gave him the verdict, "Alright, Levi, you and your family have been trying very hard. It doesn't seem fair to foreclose without giving you another chance. You won't have to make your payment this year, but next year you'll have to make two payments, $600.00."

That sounded impossible, but Pa had no choice but to agree. When Pa came back into the house, we all silently stared at him, afraid to hear his report. Knowing Pa, I think he toyed with the thought of telling us to get ready to move. But he just couldn't do that to us.

Finally, he said it all in two words, "We're staying!" You can imagine the response. We kids jumped around, yelling and screaming. But the best of all was to see Ma and Pa hugging while tears of joy covered their cheeks.

Thankfully, we prayed and worked even harder during that next year. We had some rain when necessary for the small grain and we were able to harvest a fair crop. We made hay for the milk cows, bought some little chickens to raise for future egg production, bought two more sows for raising pigs, and paid the $600.00 farm payment when it was due! Oh, how thankful we were for the Lord's blessing. Finally, we would not have to move again in the near future. We could make this our home.

The Cat Man

We didn't know his name. We didn't know where he came from. One day, there he was—unshaven, rather small and thin. He appeared out in the barn while we were doing chores. Pa spoke to him and welcomed him to our farm. The little man curiously looked about in our barn. He asked a number of questions about any pets we might have. He spoke softly, almost in a whisper.

Particularly, he wanted to know if we had any cats. Cats were never a favorite in our family. We had dogs, but we never wished for a cat as a pet. We thought of them mainly as mice-catchers. It seems that cats would come and go. We might see one in the barn or in the yard, from time to time, but we never did much to encourage them to stay. And usually they didn't.

After a while the small, thin, unshaven, soft-spoken man apparently was satisfied with what he saw. For then came the reason for his visit. He asked if he could bring a few cats to our place. Pa inquired, "How many is 'a few'?"

The little man assured Pa, "Probably three or four." Pa always had a difficult time saying "no" if someone asked for a favor. As Pa considered his offer, the man promised to take care of them and feed them regularly. He even promised to furnish the "milch," as he called it. Of course, Pa agreed to permit the man to bring out a few cats.

The next day, he arrived with boxes in his old car. The back seat was full; the trunk was full. One by one he carried the boxes into the barn. As he opened the boxes out jumped the cats. There were two—four—eight—*twelve* cats that jumped out of the boxes. There were black and white cats, gold and white cats, gray ones, black ones, white ones. Some hesitated and seemed frightened as they were turned loose in the barn. Others ran up the posts and into the hay loft. They seemed to be investigating every corner of their new "home."

Since we didn't know the name of this gentle little man, we didn't know how to refer to him among ourselves. After some discussion of his particular features—his small, thin, unshaven face and soft, whispering voice, as well as his love for cats—we all agreed with little debate that his name would be, simply, "The Cat Man." He not only liked cats and took very good care of them, but frankly, there was a very strong resemblance.

It was amazing how the number of cats grew. We started with a "few," but after some weeks, there were cats everywhere. Little cats, big cats, furry cats, sleek cats, mother cats, tom cats! We were sure that the mouse population must have dropped drastically. Where did all of these cats come from? They couldn't have reproduced that fast! Could they? As time went on the mystery was solved. We discovered that slyly, like a cat, the cat man was secretly bringing more and more cats to our place. He found strays or cats that people didn't want and he became their "savior." Our barn became their haven.

Did Pa have the heart to tell The Cat Man that they were becoming a terrible nuisance? Of course not!

When we milked cows they crowded around us, hardly permitting us to walk. Their endless chorus of "meowing" was severely trying our patience. As time went on, we began to notice that some were beginning to look rather gaunt and sickly. We knew that it was not for lack of food and "milch." The Cat Man was taking very good care of them. What should we do? What should Pa do? What should The Cat Man do? We knew. But we also were convinced that Pa wouldn't do it.

Then one day, something happened that brought the matter to a head. Ma had gone to the barn for a garden tool. She hadn't noticed as one of the cats drew closer and closer to her. It was a rather sickly-looking cat. Suddenly, it lunged at her and bit her on the leg. She screamed and the cat ran away. With blood running down her leg, she came hurrying into the house and began to clean and bandage the ugly wound.

It was easily decided that Ma should see a doctor immediately. We were aware of the possibility of rabies. The doctor treated the wound and sent her home with some very definite instructions. First of all, we were to try to find the cat. Why? We were to have the cat examined to determine if it was infected with rabies. If Ma had been infected with rabies from the cat bite and nothing was done, she would likely get sick, become delirious, and eventually die.

Ma could be vaccinated for rabies. It would be a series of fourteen weekly shots in the stomach muscle. But it had to be started immediately. I was sick inside. If only we could find that cat, kill it and take it in for examination. But how? It happened so fast that Ma did not so much as remember what color it was. I pictured in my mind what it would be like if Ma wouldn't take the treatment. What if she had been infected? What if she would get rabies? I couldn't stand the thought of Ma bearing the possible long-suffering, the delirium, and finally the genuine possibility of her dying.

There were some tense hours as we searched everywhere far and wide. After we came up with nothing, we all agreed that Ma would have to undergo the treatment. There simply was no other choice. Ma systematically endured the weekly shots. We will never know if she was infected or not. Thank God, Ma remained healthy. She was a precious gift of God. She was with us until we all became adults and gave her grandchildren.

As for the cats, Pa finally informed The Cat Man that he

could not bring any more cats to our place. Furthermore, Pa urged him to find some other place for his cats. It took some time, but eventually they were all gone. As for The Cat Man, he appeared one last time in my life.

Many years later, as my wife and I greeted the guests at our wedding reception, I couldn't believe my eyes. Who should be pushing his way through the crowd—never mind the reception line—but that small, thin, unshaven, gentle little man with catlike features—The Cat Man. As he took my hand and began to speak, I bent down and turned my ear towards his rather cat-like mouth. All I could hear was a gentle and soft, "meow." I took that as "congratulations" and I thanked him for coming.

Clothes Washing Days

Putt—putt—putt—putt—One could hear it anywhere in the yard. We had a gas-powered washing machine. It was located in a small room connected to the house. No muffler. A straight, very noisy exhaust pipe vented out through a hole in the wall to the outside.

Sometimes Ma had to push the foot pedal again and again and again in an effort to start the engine. And sometimes it just wouldn't start. But Ma was ready to wash clothes. When Ma was ready, she was ready! That meant a lot of things were ready.

In the summer, we collected rain water which ran off the roof of the house into a barrel. "It is such nice, 'soft' water," Ma often commented. There was good reason why she was so happy about the "soft" water. Our well water was "hard" as a rock! When washed in the hard water the clothes never did get clean. So we were very careful to save as much rain water as we could.

The day before wash day, we carried the water into the house bucket by bucket and emptied it into the large boiler on the kitchen stove. Ma already had a good hot fire going in the cook stove. It didn't matter if it was summer or winter. The water had to be heated and there was only one way to do it at our place, on the kitchen stove. The cow chips from the pasture and the coal from the railroad generated a lot of heat.

The kitchen became very hot on wash day in the summertime. The water had to be boiling hot. Ma never let me near it as she carefully dipped the boiling water into a bucket and poured it into the wash machine.

In the winter, it was different. We had no water in the rain barrel, but we usually had mountains of white crystals on the yard. We started to gather snow about three days before wash day. We brought it into the house in buckets and dumped it into the large boiler on the stove. It melted slowly. Little by little we got a boiler full of "soft" water. When it was finally full, Ma stoked the fire and put extra chips and coal in the cook stove to bring the water to a boil.

The house got nice and warm on those days, and it was also very humid. With the air filled with moisture the windows all frosted over with crystals about one-fourth of an inch thick. We had fun drawing designs on the frosty windows until our fingers started to hurt from the cold.

After a couple of days of melting snow, we were ready to wash clothes. With a bucket, Ma dipped the water from the boiler with great care. The first reason for being careful was that it was boiling hot. The second reason was that each snowflake carried with it a speck of dirt. The specks of dirt all settled to the bottom of the boiler. Ma was careful not to disturb them.

The soap was ready too. That had been prepared previously after butchering. What did making soap have to do with butchering? Well, you see, soap was made from rendered lard from the hog that we butchered. Lye was added to the lard and amazingly, we had soap! Lye would eat holes in garments by itself, but when added to lard, it became an effective soap for removing dirt and soil from clothes. The soap was cut into small pieces so it would dissolve more quickly in the very hot water. So you see, when Ma was ready to wash clothes, everything had better work!

But what if it didn't? Did that stop our Mom? No siree. If the engine on the wash machine wouldn't start, I knew what Plan B was. It was the wooden backup wash machine with a handle. Pushing the handle back and forth, back and forth, was my job. This turned the gears and made the agitator of the wash machine rotate back and forth much like many of the modern ones do today. If this old machine hadn't been used for a time, of course, the wood dried out and we had more of a watery mess on the floor than usual. Needless to say, I was always very happy when the motor started on the wash machine.

Ringing the soapy water out of the clothes was the next job. If the engine didn't start, we fastened a hand-cranked clothes ringer on the edge of the wash machine and ran the wet clothes through the rubber rollers of the ringer. Once again, this was a job that usually fell to me. From there, the clothes fell into the rinsing tub which contained clean water. The ringer was then fastened to the side of the rinsing tub and the clothes were once again run through the rubber rollers. This time they fell into the clothes basket sitting in my wagon. This was repeated over and over again until all the clothes were washed.

Whew! What a job!

So when the engine on the washing machine started, I jumped up and down with joy. There was a ringer on the machine run by the engine. It made the job much easier, but it could be dangerous. The shrill yell of my sister, Viola, one day proved that. As she reached down into the tub to get some of the last pieces of clothing her long, flowing hair got caught in the ringer and was gradually pulling her head toward the rubber rollers. She screamed, I yelled, and Ma came running and hit the panic lever. I just stood watching wondering what would happen if the panic lever wouldn't work.

The rest was easy, especially in the summertime. I helped Ma get the clothes out to the clothes line with my wagon, but the clothes line was too high for me, so I just played while Ma hung them on the line. In the winter, when the weather was not very nice, the clothes

were hung on lines strung across the rooms in the house. But if the weather permitted, they were hung out even in the winter. It was funny when Ma brought them in after they had frozen stiff. They were all like cardboard clothes.

Wash day was a lot of work, especially for my Ma. She worked so hard every day from early morning until late at night. She was such a loving, hard-working mother. She did everything she could to care for her family. I often wonder if we, her family, did what we could to make her life easier or at least let her know how much we appreciated her seemingly tireless labor for her family. Ma had it right when she repeated what was so very true, "The men, they work from sun to sun. The woman's work is never done." At the time, I fear, we may not have appreciated her family dedication as we should have. But we loved her very much and I am sure she knew that.

Harvest Time

There is nothing more beautiful to the South Dakota farmer than the "Amber waves of grain" or a herd of cattle grazing in the spring's lush pasture grass with newborn calves romping about. I for one am thankful that I had the privilege of growing up in South Dakota with all of the trials, challenges, and joys of farm life in the 1930's and 40's.

One of the times of year that carries many happy memories is harvest time. What a great time of the year! All year long, we watched and prayed as the grain in the field continued to struggle against the drought and the grasshoppers and the weeds, not to mention the hail storms. Finally, whether there was a poor, average, or good crop, it was time for harvest.

The golden grain waving in the wind was beautiful to behold. One could see the gracious loving hand of God caring for His creation in every field of grain.

I never ceased to marvel at what was originally called the Self-Binder. We called it, simply, the Binder. It came out of the years of the industrial revolution, and it was an amazing machine. Even though it was invented in the latter part of the 19th century, it was still in use in our area until the mid-20th century. At that time, it, together with the threshing machine, was replaced with the combine.

The amazing Binder, which was originally ground-driven and pulled by horses, cut the grain, elevated it up to the tying deck on a canvas escalator, packed the grain stalks until there was enough to make a bundle, automatically wrapped twine around the bundle, tied it up, cut the twine, and "kicked" the bundle out to land on the bundle carrier. It was an amazing operation! I simply marveled at the engineering of this machine that performed intricate tasks over and over again with seldom a mistake. Before the binder was invented, the farmers cut the grain and tied each bunch of grain into a bundle by hand. One can imagine how thankful the farmers were for such a "high-tech" piece of equipment.

The Binder was invented to be a one-man operation. When it was adapted to be pulled by a tractor it required two people. One person drove the tractor—that was me when I was ten years of age. Another person, in this case, Pa, rode on the Binder and "tripped" the bundle carrier at the same places each time as we rotated around the field. This placed the piles of bundles all in a row.

After the grain in a field was all cut and the bundles all lay in neat rows across the field, it was a picture to behold. But the picture lost some of its charm as we realized that it was time for shocking. I felt that there was a good reason why it was called "shocking." There was probably nothing more shocking and overwhelming to me, as a young man of ten years of age, than to come out to an 80 acre field to begin shocking. The rows of bundles all lying in parallel rows across the field was like a symmetrical work of art. But when looking at the fields from the laborers' point of view, the rows appeared endless! It seemed like it would take a year to get it all done!

Eighty to one hundred acres of thousands of bundles lay there waiting to be picked up, two bundles at a time, leaning them against each other, adding more, to finally form a kind of tepee-looking shock. Down one row and over to the next we went until the field was all shocked and waiting to be threshed. What a job! But there was always a feeling of accomplishment when one finally finished a field and stepped back to recognize the generous blessing of our gracious God.

Aaron VanNuys

As we gradually emerged from the great depression of the 1930's, our machinery was mostly horse-drawn. Repairs were difficult to find. After WW II began, it was almost impossible to find the necessary parts to repair our old machinery. Tractors with power driven machinery were dominating the production of farm machinery. Besides that many of the factories were converted to take part in the war effort. There was no complaining because of that. We all knew that the war was necessary. We felt that we wanted to do whatever we could to help, be it ever so slight. So we learned to make do with what we had.

Our local welder was kept quite busy. However, it didn't take much to do that because Aaron was not highly motivated. He was a kind and gentle man in his early thirties. He lived in a tiny house in the little village of Kampeska, a couple of miles from Lake Kampeska, near Watertown. Aaron was a dead ringer for Pa Kettle from the movies featuring Ma and Pa Kettle. Though everything was falling apart and needed fixing, Pa Kettle's famous promise was, "I've gotta fix that one of these days." Well, of course, he never did. Aaron didn't either.

Aaron was never in a hurry. Plenty of time. No stress. He even talked slowly, as though every word was an effort. It didn't matter how many broken pieces people brought to him to weld, he moved at the same pace—slow, very slow. But he was the only welder for miles around and a good one at that.

Aaron's yard was strewn with old pieces of equipment and metal parts of all kinds. One just never knew when one might need a piece of metal to reinforce a broken grain binder, hay rake, mower, etc.

One day, as we were just beginning to harvest the oats, we broke a sprocket on our grain binder. Actually, Pa broke it while trying to "adjust" something else with the hammer. So there we were at Aaron's place with our broken gear in hand.

It was mid-afternoon as we knocked on the door. We knocked and knocked until finally Aaron came to the door. Clearly, he had settled in for a good afternoon nap. He came to the door squinting and brushing his hair back out of his face as Pa explained our predicament.

"Well...I don't know," Aaron answered Pa in his usual ultra-slow drawl. "I've...got a couple of... pieces here…ahead of you." There was silence as Aaron looked down at the steps in front of his house. Finally, without a word, Aaron grabbed a cap from behind his door and emerged from his house pulling his welder's cap tightly over his partly balding head. "It could be… a couple of days…ya know … before … I can…get at it," Aaron offered, rather thoughtfully.

I looked at Pa. He had this mischievous grin on his face. I just knew that Pa would not give up that easily. I wondered what Pa would say next.

"Well," Pa responded, "I'll tell you what we'll do Aaron. We'll wait."

Aaron looked rather startled as he quickly glanced at Pa. He looked down at the ground and kicked a piece of metal. Finally, he said, "I don't know…Levi …I have these other…two pieces…to get out."

As politely as possible, Pa repeated, "That's okay Aaron, we'll wait." Then, as though to emphasize his decision, Pa grabbed an old, five-gallon paint pail, tipped it upside down, and sat on it.

Aaron walked about aimlessly, eyeing Pa from time to time. Finally, Aaron picked up the sprocket and headed into his welding shed. In twenty minutes he returned with the welding finished.

"Good job," Pa complimented. After cooling it in a tub of rain water, Aaron handed it over to Pa. Pa questioned, "How much?"

"Well," Aaron drawled, "I have to...charge you...$1.50, Levi. I had to hurry, you know."

Pa thanked him and paid him. We couldn't help but have a good laugh as we went down the road back to the grain field. Aaron VanNuys was a very well-known and greatly needed part of our community. We felt very fortunate to have him in the neighborhood. But I am sure that he could have played the part of Pa Kettle without a bit of coaching.

Threshing Time

It was time for the annual threshing meeting! I always looked forward to it. Threshing the grain was one of the great high points of the year. Finally, the fruits of our labors were about to be gathered into our granaries. But first, the neighboring farmers had to talk about it. As a young lad, I enjoyed going along with Pa to the threshing meetings. Besides listening to the farmers plan their work, some of the wives came along to visit. Best of all, the ladies always prepared a sumptuous lunch after the meeting.

The farmers worked out a plan of cooperation. They organized a yearly threshing "run," which established the order for moving from one farmer's place to another to thresh their grain, convey it to their granary, or haul it to the local elevator. One farmer owned a threshing rig (a threshing machine and tractor) while the other farmers furnished bundle wagons, grain wagons, a grain elevator, horses, and manpower. They organized things so that each farmer would get two days of threshing time on the first "run." After that was finished, they started again, at the beginning, and finished threshing whatever was left for each farmer.

When I was about ten years old I was already helping Pa on the threshing run. Pa couldn't work very much because of his increasingly difficult asthmatic condition, so he and I were counted as one man. We hauled the grain away from the threshing machine in grain wagons pulled with a team of horses and shoveled it into the elevator at the farmer's granary. The grain went up the elevator and dropped into a bin in the granary to be stored for feed, seed for the following year, or selling at a future time. Pa kept me out of school to help with the harvest. I didn't mind at all. I liked being around the horses and machinery as well as listening to the men discuss various subjects and kid each other about one thing or another. The schools of that day accepted one's absence around harvest time as not out of the ordinary. Of course, I always had heaps of makeup work to do when I finally returned to school.

Twelve o'clock noon always offered a special experience with the threshing crew. Wherever we were working, that farmer's wife and their daughters were responsible for dinner. What an experience! The women worked very hard. Many were still using wood or coal-burning cook stoves. They had to prepare for 12–14 hungry men for dinner. Then there were the afternoon snacks brought out to the field. Usually, the snacks and meals were delicious.

We each washed our face and hands at the makeshift, outdoor water basin next to the water pump by the well. For some reason there was always only one towel. If one happened to wash last—and I usually did—the towel was rather wet. But I used it anyway, not wanting to be different. It probably was no worse than all of us drinking out of the same water can with the same dipper! Our immune systems must have worked overtime.

We filed into the house. There, the dining room table was spread with delicious food from end to end. What a feast! This was usually topped off with some type of pie or cake. I loved it! But there were times…

One place where no one wanted to eat was at the Carlson's. Their small home was not at all clean. The twelve children were rowdy and smelled like they needed baths badly. This was detectable even in the company of a dozen sweaty, hard-working men. Carlson's teenage and very overweight daughter, Lena, had long, straggly, unwashed hair that hung unkempt over her face.

Pa was a real teaser. One day before we went in to dinner at Carlson's, Pa was teasing some of the fellow workers about getting one of Lena's long hairs in their food. Again, the dinner was not a very pleasant experience. No one talked at the table. All seemed to be concentrating upon eating and probably thinking about what Pa had teasingly said.

But then, one by one, all of the men turned their eyes toward Pa. As he carefully ate his dinner that day, all of a sudden, he began to discreetly touch his lips. Obviously, he was trying to remove a hair from his mouth without anyone noticing! They noticed! The more he pulled, the longer it proved to be. Finally, he was pulling it out hand over hand. It must have been 18 inches long! There were lots of snickers around the table. But, no one said a word.

When dinner was over and we went outside, there was no end to the ribbing and joshing that Pa had to endure. He had it coming. After making an issue of it by his teasing, he deserved every bit of it. No one forgot this incident. The threshing crew tried everything they knew to avoid eating at the Carlson's. If there was a half day's work left, they worked feverishly to finish before noon. Our farm was always next on the "run." With horses galloping, they tried to make it to our place just in time for dinner! This happened more than once, so Ma was prepared and ready to serve.

A Boy and
A Man's Job

Why would Pa ask a boy to do a man's job? Well, there were reasons. In the first place, we were short-handed. With World War II came the shortage of manpower in many aspects of production. Though a few transit workers were available and sometimes hired, still there was a shortage. I liked to go to town with Pa when he went to hire workers. There the young men were, standing on street corners, waiting for a job opportunity.

Many of them were farm boys from some of the southern states that had already finished their harvest. They traveled north to help with the harvest and earn a few dollars. $4.00 a day was the going wage. They didn't mind sleeping in the barn in a straw stall. They always ate with us. Some became a matter of great interest to my two sisters. The idea of them being from a far-off place like Oklahoma or Kansas was tremendously intriguing to them. Their slight southern drawl was a definite plus.

But now we were getting to the end of the threshing season and most of the transit workers were gone.

But we had another problem. A serious disagreement arose between one of the farmers and the engineer of the threshing rig. I can still see it all in my mind. It was early in the morning. Bernard, the engineer, was greasing, checking, and generally preparing his rig for the day. Carl, one of the farmers, came tearing into our yard with dust flying! He jumped out of his car, slammed the door, and headed for the threshing rig. As he approached the rig, he angrily began yelling. Bernard didn't so much as look up. Apparently, Carl was convinced that he was not getting his share of threshing time and was threatening to leave the "run." I thought to myself, *Why now, when we are so close to the end?*

Finally, Bernard had enough. He stood up and said with unmistaken clarity, (His exact words I will not repeat) "If you don't like the gate we're swingin' on, then get off!" With that, Bernard turned around and continued preparing his machine for a day of threshing. Carl continued to yell unmentionable words over his shoulder as he strutted back to his car and left our yard in a cloud of dust. In brief: We were suddenly short another man.

My older brother and I were kept out of school to help with the harvest. I was once again helping Pa haul grain and my brother was already pitching bundles. I was somewhat envious of my brother. Pitching bundles seemed to be a definite sign of manhood. Even though my brother and I were three years apart in age, we were about the same size. Nevertheless, I didn't feel ready for that kind of responsibility. After the very loud vocal disagreement in our yard Pa came over to where we were standing. He told us what we already had gathered. "We're short a man for a bundle rack." I started to feel somewhat uncomfortable because Pa looked straight at me when he spoke. But I was really surprised when he continued, "Would you like to try it?"

One might wonder how Pa, so easily, could keep us out of school to help with the farm work. It was not as though he didn't care if we got an education or not. He was all for us going to school. He proved that without question when he sold Bessie to help with my sister's education. Yet, regular attendance in school never appeared to be a priority with Pa.

But we need to be fair to Pa. He was a product of his time. As a boy, Pa went to school during the winter months when there was absolutely nothing else to do. As a result, it took him many years to progress as far as he did. He readily admitted that he quit school when he was eighteen years of age and in the third grade. Pa jokingly, but truthfully, acknowledged that, finally, he and the teacher were the same age. In Pa's typical sense of humor, he kidded that it might have been proper for him to date his teacher rather than be her student. I am sure it was somewhat humiliating for Pa to squeeze into those small desks and have someone his age try to teach him how to read and write. As a result, he wanted his children to get an education but it was not a terribly serious matter to him.

For a young man (or boy), it was admittedly rather challenging to be considered to do a man's job. But pitching bundles? That involved some rather intense work, a certain amount of pressure, and handling a team of horses close to the threshing machine. I was tall for my age, but only 12 years old!

There were six bundle haulers. Along the rows of shocks we went, pitching the bundles into the bundle wagon, sometimes two bundles at a time. A good team of horses followed the row of shocks and started and stopped by voice signals. "Getty-up—Whoa." When the bundle wagon was stacked full, as high as one could throw them, then one climbed on top and leveled them off a bit, threw on a few more, and guided the horses up to the threshing machine.

What a job that was! The horses didn't like it at all! Even with blinders on their bridles, which somewhat shielded their side vision, they could see and hear enough to cause them to be very reluctant to pull up closely to the machine. The whirring of belts and chains, the swishing of the wheels, the noise of the motor of the tractor and the threshing machine, not to mention the heavy cloud of grain dust and straw particles in the air all around the machine—I was always fearful that as they switched flies with their tail they easily could catch it in a chain or pulley. What a ride we would be in for then!

Each time I approached the machine, I could detect fear in the body language of the horses. They were fidgety and fought to stay a safe distance from the machine. But the farther they pulled away from the bundle feeder, the more difficult it was for the bundle pitcher. I certainly didn't need that! The horses never got used to it. Neither did I!

The temperature was very high that day as I began my first day on the job of bundle pitching. It was ninety degrees Fahrenheit by noon. I was falling behind, hardly managing to keep my place in the rotation of bundle haulers. If I didn't continue to bring in a full load of bundles it would cause the other haulers to have to work all the harder. I didn't want that to happen. Even though no one said a word to me, I felt the pressure. I loaded and unloaded without stopping to rest or get a drink of water. That was a mistake.

There was only one way that the bundle haulers could get time to rest. That was accomplished by "plugging" the threshing machine. This was done by throwing more bundles into the feeder of the machine than it could "digest," so to speak. Since Bernard's tractor, which powered the machine, was barely adequate, a few extra bundles would cause it to grunt and groan, lose momentum and finally the machine gave one last sound, "chunk" and the drive belt would go flying off the drive pulley and everything stopped!

Most bundle haulers considered the engineer to have it pretty easy. When everything worked well he seemed to simply wander about, checking a few things, squirting a little oil here and there. But often he was leaning on a pitch fork or resting comfortably against a shock of grain. So the bundle haulers were not above planning a little rest of their own by "accidentally" overloading the threshing machine and finally "plugging" it. You see, getting it running again was solely the job of the engineer!

As I was working feverishly loading my bundle rack to keep my place in the rotation, suddenly the distant noise of the threshing rig came to an abrupt stop. The straw was no longer spewing out of the straw pipe. All was silent. What happened?

As I came in with my load of bundles there was Bernard half way into the under-side of the machine amidst the dust and chaff pulling the wads of straw out of the threshing cylinder. I could only imagine what had happened. The bundle pitchers were all over by the water can seeming to enjoy their little respite. Did the bundle hauler who preceded me in rotation do this on purpose? Did he do it for my sake? I never found out. For who is going to own up to that? Anyway, it was a good rest. I even had time to get a drink of water.

Nevertheless, the heat was taking it's toll. By noon I wasn't feeling well at all. I ate very little. Again, no one said anything to me but I knew that the other bundle haulers were having to work faster because I was not holding up my end of it. After dinner, it was really hot. I tried to keep up, but finally I was too sick and too weak to work. I had a headache and became dizzy and sick to my stomach. I learned later that I was having a sun stroke. I found a shady place in the doorway of the barn where the breeze was passing through and tried to relax.

I was physically sick but I felt even worse emotionally because I had failed in my very first real test on a man's job. When I had the strength to walk, I went home and left the team of horses and wagon in case someone would find a way to use them. I helped Ma with the evening chores of milking, hog feeding, etc. Ma didn't ask any questions. When Pa came home, he didn't mention the matter either. That was ok. I talked especially long to the Lord my Savior that night, thanking Him for keeping me safe and well. I felt better after prayer and had a good night's sleep.

The next day I went to school. As I walked to school on that nice autumn day, I was happy. I had learned some things about myself and how better to deal with difficulties in life. Actually, I was glad to be going to school. That was something that I could do. That was good. It was where I belonged.

The Horse vs. The Tractor

"Levi, are you still buying horses?" Pa heard that a lot after he bought a team of strawberry roan Belgians. To the farmers of Pa's generation, having good horses was a sign of progress and success. In those days, "horsepower" was literally horse power. A good farmer had to have it. And a good farmer had good horses.

As I was growing up, tractors were becoming ever more popular. Horses were becoming extinct as the primary source of power on the farm. But Pa loved horses. When others were looking at the latest tractor models, Pa was still looking at horses.

One of Pa's friends, Oscar, who was a prosperous farmer, had always owned some of the finest horses. But now he was giving them up and going the way of progress—a tractor and the necessary equipment to go with it.

One day, Pa decided to go and visit Oscar. It was about 20 miles. That seemed like such a long way. It was especially long when Pa was driving. Pa never drove very fast. Sometimes, being deep in thought, he drove and hummed, never getting the car shifted out of second gear. So driving 20 miles might take more than an hour. But that was okay with me. I was happy to be riding along and watching the farmers in the fields and the livestock in the pastures.

Finally, we arrived at Oscar's place. The yard and the buildings were well kept. Oscar was in the yard. He came over to the car.

"Well, hello, Levi. Nice to see you," Oscar cordially welcomed.

After Oscar and Pa had chatted awhile, Pa inquired, "I heard that you were selling your horses. Do you have any good ones left?"

"Well, yes," Oscar replied. "I am keeping one team, but I have an excellent team of strawberry roan Belgians that I would sell to someone who will take good care of them."

Oscar led us to the yard. There they were, next to a hayrack, devouring hay like threshing machines. I had never seen such big horses. They were huge! Pa asked about their age, their weight, and other horse details.

"Yep, Levi, they weigh over a ton each. They're only eight years old, and I'll guarantee that team can pull anything that's loose," Oscar proudly answered.

We really didn't need horses that big! After all, we weren't going to plow with them! We would be using them for haying, hauling bundles at threshing time, and work like that.

Oscar pointed out, "Dick is the feisty one. Barney is more calm and steady." Immediately, Pa fell in love with them, huge as they were. He gave Oscar a few dollars and promised to pay the balance as soon as possible. Oscar agreed. They shook hands and we left.

Pa was so proud of his strawberry roan Belgians. But the neighbors ribbed Pa continually. After all, when everyone was visiting the implement dealers and trying to buy used or new tractors, Pa went and bought another team of horses—big horses that were bred for doing heavy work! Big horses that did heavy eating and drinking. In the winter, we couldn't keep their manger full of hay. They ate oats by the buckets-full and drank water a gallon per swallow. But Pa loved them.

One cold, wintry day, we had just finished doing chores, which included taking care of Pa's precious horses, when the telephone rang. The telephone lines had been installed the summer before. By late fall, we decided to pay the two dollars per month and have a telephone installed. It was still new to us and when the telephone rang we all got excited. Who could it be? It was a party line so your business was everybody's business. Though everyone knew, no one seemed to mind very much that listening to other people's conversations was a well-known pastime for many of the farmers' wives. After all, what better way to find out the latest happenings in the neighborhood?

Ma answered. It was for Pa. Pa listened for a long time without saying a word. Finally he answered, "Well, we'll see what we can do. We'll be there after dinner." Pa came away from the telephone with a kind of smirk on his face. He explained that Bill, the manager of the grain elevator in the little village of Kampeska, needed some help. The grain elevator that Bill managed was a farmer co-op. As a service to the neighborhood, Bill handled coal. The coal cars were

parked by the coal bins. They were then unloaded by hand with a shovel. My brother, Charles, and I unloaded some of the coal cars from time to time. He got $4.00 to unload one car of coal into the bins. It took all day.

Sometimes Bill would order more coal cars than could be parked by the coal bins. As they were emptied, Bill had to move the empty cars and get someone to help move the full ones into place. Since tractors were becoming more common and the owners made big claims about what they could do with them, Bill called on farmers to help him move the coal cars when it was necessary.

This time, Bill called a number of farmers to help him. Some tried but failed. The ground was frozen and covered with snow and ice. The tractors just couldn't get traction with their rubber tires and they were not able to do the job. Bill remembered that Pa had recently bought a team of big Belgians. Could they possibly do the job? Well, when Bill called Pa, how could he refuse? After all, Pa had been ridiculed and laughed at by many of the neighbors, some of whom had come with tractors to move the coal cars and were not able.

Pa bundled up and went out into the freezing cold to harness the horses. I bundled up too. I had to go along and see this! Pa hitched them to the sleigh, I climbed in, and off we went over and through the deep drifts. Dick and Barney plowed through the snow with reckless abandon, seeming to enjoy that for which they were bred, namely, pulling something, anything!

We arrived at the elevator and Bill was out by the coal bins. He was glad to see Pa and remarked, "Man, Levi, that is one huge team of horses."

"Yea," Pa responded proudly. "We'll see if they're big enough for this job."

Pa and Bill decided where to place the horses so they could get the best footing. Pa used his best evener, the wooden contraption that caused the horses to pull evenly. They fastened two heavy log chains to the evener and then to the coal car. Pa gently signaled to the team to get them into position and tighten the tugs.

The tugs were tight. Pa glanced at me and motioned for me to get farther back in case something would break. Pa quickly visually inspected everything to make sure it all checked out. Then with a confident look, he gave the driving reins a firm, quick snap and shouted, "Getty Yup!"

Dick and Barney stretched into the pull. Dick slipped some on the hard, frozen ground, but he quickly recovered. Now they both put their entire two-plus tons of weight into it. Their muscles quivered. I felt so sorry for them. It must have been the toughest pull they ever had. The car didn't budge. Tears began to trickle down my checks as I watched them pull so hard that Dick dropped to his knees. But right then the wheels of the coal car began to move ever so slightly. Dick and Barney felt it immediately. Dick was up on all four legs in an instant and gradually the car began to roll into position.

Cars going by had stopped along the road to watch. Some blew their horns. Others watching began to shout and clap their glove-covered hands. As cold as it was, I was warm all over. Dick and Barney seemed to sense a great accomplishment as Pa went to their heads and petted them and talked gently to them.

The word spread through the neighborhood. It was amazing. Suddenly all the ribbing and ridicule about Pa buying those big Belgians was no longer heard. During the neighborhood threshing runs, Dick and Barney were highly respected as a team that just wouldn't quit. And Pa was not about to let anyone forget the day when his horses showed up the tractors in the community.

Every other job we had for Dick and Barney was like a walk in the park. A load of bundles or hay was nothing. A wagon load of grain—they hardly noticed they were pulling anything. While dragging a car through the snow-blocked roads in winter or the muddy roads in the spring, they never broke a sweat. What a team of horses!

But, finally, the tractor was victorious. The horses may have won a battle now and then, but the tractor won the war, as the saying goes. The horse became obsolete as the primary power on the farm. This made many, including Pa, very sad. Nevertheless, it was inevitable, I suppose. It's called progress.

After years of watching Dick and Barney graze lazily in the pasture and caring for them through the winter, they were sold for very little. But I will never forget that one day of triumph when Dick and Barney won the battle between the horse and the tractor.

N. T. Nelson

"Oh no! N.T. is coming," Ma blurted out as she peered through the frosty kitchen window pane on what was a very cold winter day. We were snowbound and certainly did not expect company. Yet, in the dead of winter, when the weather was the coldest, we often did get a visitor. His name was N.T. Nelson.

Pa was a friend to everyone. As a result, there were people, from time to time, who seemed to have no family or friends, yet they were befriended by Pa. One such individual was N.T. Nelson. He never talked to us children. He and Pa didn't talk much either, most of the time. They just sat in the living room. Pa put in a chew of Copenhagen, rocked in his rocking chair, hummed some tune not known to anyone but himself, and spit in his spittoon. N.T. often just sat across the room in another rocking chair and dozed. Sometimes Pa offered N.T. a "pinch" of Copenhagen. It was fun to watch as he took a "pinch" and snuffed it up into his nose. I wondered, *how does he keep from sneezing?*

I thought Copenhagen smelled good. I was curious about how it must taste. As a young lad, I asked Pa how it tasted. He opened the round, tin-covered container and reached it out to me, seeming to dare me to try some. I think he was surprised when I placed a finger into the soft ground tobacco. My finger picked up a few crumbs and I touched my tongue with my finger. Ugh! It was sharp and sickening. Immediately my stomach started to churn and I felt ill. I ran to the sink and spit and spit and spit! I couldn't believe how sick I felt from just a crumb or two on my tongue. Pa just smiled. He had accomplished what he had hoped for. I never touched tobacco in any form from that day on.

But back to N.T. He lived about a mile from our place on eighty acres of very hilly and rocky land. He had two or three head of cattle and a goat or two. About 300 yards from the dirt road that went by his place were a few very small shacks and old car bodies randomly "parked" here and there. N.T. slept in a car body, even in the winter. It might seem difficult to believe, but all he had for heat and light was a kerosene lantern. If the wick of the lantern wasn't trimmed properly it gave off a great deal of smoke. We could always tell when his lantern wasn't working well—N.T. would arrive at our house with his face and hands as black as tar!

It was not unusual, but never expected, to see N.T. plodding through the snow drifts with walking stick in hand, making his way to our place in the dead of winter. The roads all might be blocked, the temperature might be twenty below zero, but there came N.T. bundled up in layers of ragged and not-so-clean clothing. His overshoes were torn and had patches upon patches. His coarse, shaggy eyebrows outlined his sharp, sunken eyes. His heavy whiskers and eyebrows were often covered with ice crystals as he was invited in from the cold. The smell of smoke that had penetrated his clothing followed him into the house.

I was always just a little excited when N.T. came. Something was happening, even though it was only a visit from N.T! When we were snowed in, the days and nights got rather long. Electricity had not yet reached our rural area. Television had not even been heard of by us. The books that we had to read were a couple of "big little" books that we had uncovered in the ol' sand pit. In them we found stories about various heroic adventures and tales about Buck Rogers and his space travels. Of course, we knew that could never happen! Other than that we listened to the battery-powered radio, whittled on a piece of wood, played games, or did some school work. We were fortunate to have an Aladdin lamp that gave more light than the regular kerosene lamps with a wick. Still, the light was rather dim and it was not easy to read and do school work at night. (At least, that was our excuse.) I often wondered how Abraham Lincoln got all of his reading done with candle light. In the day time, besides chores like gathering eggs, feeding the chickens, and taking care of the livestock in general, we spent our time sledding on the snow and trying to skate on a frozen puddle near our house.

So, when N.T. came, at least it was something different. He liked to talk about his religious ideas. He claimed to be a Jehovah's Witness, so we had the opportunity to share with him our faith and tell him about our Savior, Jesus Christ, and how He saved us from our sins. Again and again he referred to the 144,000 mentioned in the book of Revelation. He believed this number to be the literal number of those who would finally be saved and go to heaven. Pa felt constrained to put N.T. on the spot regarding his beliefs.

Everyone in the room stopped what they were doing when Pa asked N.T. directly, "What do you think, N.T.? Will I be one of the 144,000?" The room was silent for some time as N.T. squirmed, rocked in his chair and stared at the floor. Finally, as though he had a revelation of some sort, he stopped rocking, sat up straight, looked Pa straight in the eyes and answered, "I think so." Well, we all breathed a sigh of relief to hear that, even though it was rather indefinite!

Surprisingly, N.T. knew a lot about what was happening in the world. He had his opinion about almost everything. The day dragged on. N.T. really didn't want any one's pity but Ma often fixed a meal for him or sent some food home with him. I think he was appreciative even though he never said anything to Ma, not even "thank you." I got the feeling that in N.T.'s way of thinking, women and children would likely not be among the 144,000!

I never could understand why N. T. stayed so long. Sometimes he stayed until eleven o'clock at night! It was dark and cold. Ma, who was the most loving and gentle person I ever knew, had made it very clear that unless there was a real reason, like sick unto death, we should never invite N.T. to stay over night. So on many dreary nights he walked more than a mile across snow banks that were three- to four-feet deep, in twenty degree below temperatures, to his "home." I tried to picture him arriving at his humble old car body, in the dead of winter, crawling inside that dingy little chamber and lighting the kerosene lantern for heat and light.

My upstairs bedroom was not heated. In the cold nights of winter the floor was icy cold and it was tough to crawl into that cold bed. We often heated a flat iron (the solid steel part of Ma's clothes iron) on the top of the cook stove, wrapped it in a towel, and put it at the foot of our bed to keep our feet warm, at least until we got to sleep. But that was nothing compared to what N.T. must have endured.

We wondered what we could do to help N.T. His land was mostly hilly and rocky. Yet there were a few small patches of ground that were tillable. So Pa and I went to see N.T. one day in the spring of the year. We wanted to see if he would like for us to try to farm a few small parcels of land for him. When we arrived, he was out in his yard by a shed trying to make a fence with old rusty wire and some sticks and dead tree branches. He had purchased a young cow and she had just given birth to a calf. How he got the money for that was a mystery. N.T. was very proud of his new addition. He seemed to be excited that he could share this special happening in his life with us, his visitors.

I suppose he felt that he should offer his guests something. He opened a door to an old shed and reached in and took a pail from a nail. He had just milked his young cow and had about a gallon of milk. He proceeded to take some cups down that were hanging on nails and poured each of us a cup of milk. As he poured, I noticed that various foreign objects floated in the milk. A couple of flies were treading milk and a couple more looked dead. There were other particles that looked like straw and some I really didn't want to think about. But N.T. meant well. He even tried to prevent some of the foreign objects from floating into the cups for his special guests.

I don't know what Pa did with his. I slyly pretended to drink and when N.T. turned his head I poured mine out on the ground. I eyed the various dark particles that remained at the bottom of the cup. I was glad that I hadn't tried to drink any of the milk. When N.T. noticed mine was gone, immediately he offered a refill. I think he was rather hurt when I graciously declined.

I farmed some of N.T.'s land for some years. It gave him a little income. But he never did vacate the car body. After many years he finally moved to what many called the "poor farm." There were no nursing homes. The county homes were the only alternative when there was no where else to go. Pa and I visited N. T. while he was there. His home, shared with many others, was a long room like an army barracks. Cots lined the walls on both sides. There was a bathroom on one end with a kitchen and a place to eat on the other. It was very basic but was far better than what N.T. had lived in for many years.

N.T. apparently had no relatives, and it seemed as though he had no friends. We were happy that he appeared to be content at the "poor house." He seemed pleased that we had come to visit him, even though he couldn't offer his guests much for hospitality, not even a cup of milk.

Snowbound

Large flakes of snow fell lazily to the ground. We were informed on the radio that a snowstorm was predicted. We hurried to get the chores done as early as possible. The cows were milked and the milk was separated. The cattle and horses were all watered and fed. The eggs were gathered and the chickens were taken care of as well as the hogs. As we finished chores, the wind was becoming more intense. By the time we got to the house, the snow was swirling around the buildings and collecting into banks. Snow continued to fall and the wind howled all night. In the morning all was white—a winter wonderland. Large banks of snow collected between the house and the barn. The road ditches disappeared beneath the white hills. The road was covered with tapered walls of white crystals two to four feet high. There was no doubt about it. We were snowbound!

It is not as though we lived out in the wilderness somewhere many miles from a main highway. Not at all. As a matter of fact, we lived only one and one fourth miles from Highway 212. That, of course, was always cleared of snow as soon as possible. The traffic demanded it. The problem was that we lived on a township road. That meant that there was hardly any traffic and absolutely no, I mean no, public maintenance. No public workers graveled the road or plowed the snow or mowed the ditches. Whatever road maintenance took place was up to the farmers in the area who used the road.

Our neighbors were not much for cooperative activities, especially things like roadwork. One was a bachelor. The other was a family man with a wife and twelve children, at last count. We worked together during harvest, but we hardly ever saw them during the winter. However, the one place where we might meet them occasionally was at Pete's Place. Pete and his wife ran a gasoline station on Highway 212 where our town-ship road met the highway. Pete also sold bread, milk, snacks, pop, beer, and various sundries.

Usually, especially in the winter, there was a card game going on in the corner. It seemed like everyone smoked, so Pete's little one-room building was usually filled with a kind of smoky haze. If we happened to stop there in the winter, our two closest neighbors were almost always there. The family man always had his wife along and they sipped on a beer and played cards all day long. They always seemed to be in a good mood. We spoke and traded a few remarks about the weather and the depth of the snow and other small talk. That was about it. After a snowstorm, our neighbors walked down to Pete's Place like any other winter day. At least, now they had something to talk about. Needless to say, road maintenance, apparently, was not one of their points of discussion. As a result, trying to keep the road to Highway 212 in passable condition was up to our family, entirely.

The road was not well drained, so in the spring and summer, after heavy rains, the road was mud—heavy, clay, stick-to-everything kind of mud! Getting stuck in the mud was even worse than trying to plow through the snowdrifts. Today it might almost seem humorous, but in those days, when people bought cars, one of the huge considerations was, "How much clearance does it have?" The ruts became so deep at times we were pushing mud with the front bumper.

When the roads were really wet and muddy, the only way to get to the highway was to hook Dick and Barney to the bumper of the car and drag it through the muddiest places. There was only one bright spot. We knew that when things dried out a little we could go to a distant neighbor, who was the township supervisor, and pick up the one piece of road equipment owned by the county, the road blade—on wheels, no less! This was a coveted job for us kids. If we bladed the ruts out of the road and did a good job the supervisor paid us $1.00. But the county blade was of no use in the snow. And even Dick and Barney had difficulty dragging our car through those two- to four-foot drifts of snow. As a result, we became snowbound at numerous times in any given winter.

Becoming snowbound didn't alarm us. In fact, it was rather comfortable. We did our chores, which took more time after a snowstorm. Feeding the livestock and watching the cattle chew their cuds in the comfort of their straw-bedded pen had a kind of gentle peace about it all. It was almost therapeutic. Sometimes Pa forgot to come in for a meal. He enjoyed the simple "activity" of observing the livestock in their comfortable winter shelter. Some might be lying down. Others might be grabbing a bite of hay from the manger and lazily devouring it. Everything was quiet and peaceful. No one was in a hurry. There was no place to go. Company was not expected, with the possible exception of N.T. Nelson.

Ma and Pa were well aware of the very real possibility of becoming snowbound. They prepared as well as possible. Supplies of coal and corncobs were piled either in the basement or near to the house. Besides that, they "put in" for the winter, as the saying went. In the late fall, after harvest, an effort was made to stock up on various necessary items to survive a few weeks of entrapment in the snow.

In early winter, we butchered a hog and smoked much of it, which included many rings of bologna and some hams. Most of this was stored deep in the grain in the granary. This sort of storage protected the hams and bologna from the rodents. It also kept the meat cold even if we should get some warm days in the winter. Besides this, Ma was a superb food preserver. She canned chicken as well as vegetables, sauce, and more. She set aside a little extra money from egg sales and "put in" large quantities of sugar and flour. Without question, we could endure quite a long spell of tough weather, if there were no emergency.

But if there were an unexpected illness or if someone got seriously injured, then what? Well, just in case, our sleigh box was prepared with a generous amount of hay or straw for warmth and comfortable riding. And, of course, the big strawberry roan horses, Dick and Barney, were always ready. They never got sick!

School attendance was not considered an emergency. We children were in complete agreement with that. However, those of us in grades 1–8 walked to school anyway. It was only a mile away. If we were in high school we had about seven miles to go. I often walked to Pete's Place hoping to catch a ride to town for high school. I usually was successful. Generally, snow was not a serious problem, no matter how deep.

However, there was a reason for special preparations. Pa had a serious asthmatic condition. In those days, there was no medication available for public use to counter-act asthma, even by prescription. Without warning, Pa was suddenly lying in a straw stall of the barn or leaning over a partition hardly able to breathe. No matter what we tried to do, it never helped. Once it started, we knew we could do nothing to keep it from developing into a life-threatening situation. Many times it became extremely frightening. In the midst of a severe attack I often wondered if Pa was going to survive.

At normal times we helped Pa into the car and took him to the doctor. The doctor's one remedy was simply to give Pa a shot of adrenalin. Within a half hour good results were already evident. But, if we were snowbound, it was a different story.

We were finishing chores. As I walked by a straw stall there was Pa, on his knees, gasping for air. My brother and I ran to the house to tell Ma. It was starting to snow again and the wind was picking up. Ma came out with us.

"Help me get Pa into the house. Then hitch up the horses," Ma uncharacteristically ordered. "I will call Doctor Clark," Ma continued. "Pray God that he is in." We had installed a telephone only a few months before. What a blessing that was!

We shuffled through the snow and over the banks with Pa leaning heavily on us. Finally, we got into the house and made Pa as comfortable as possible, leaving the details to Ma. "Go," Ma directed firmly.

The leather harnesses were cold and stiff. With some difficulty we managed to get those two huge horses harnessed. Finally, we fastened the last tugs to the evener. As we left the barn where the sleigh was stored, we noticed that the wind was becoming more intense. The drifting snow was filling the air. The crevices in the ever-growing hills of snow were being filled. As we approached the house Ma came out and yelled, "Doctor Clark will be at Pete's Place as soon as possible."

The horses, who normally didn't do much in the winter, seemed to enjoy getting out into the deep snow. They were doing their thing—pulling something. Their huge, 2000-pound frames plunged

through the drifts. My brother and I were enjoying the ride but were, many times, on the brink of overturning as we slid off the side of a huge snowdrift only to hit another. It was a long one and one fourth miles. Finally, we were at Pete's Place. We tied the horses to a post and went inside.

Doctor Clark wasn't there yet. But, of course, there were our neighbors, sitting at a card table in a smoky haze with a bottle of beer in front of each of them. We leaned against the bar. Pete came over and asked if he could help us with something. My brother thanked him but told him why we were there. Pete became concerned and soon our neighbors noticed us and wondered why we were out on such a blustery day. They all stopped playing cards and talked to us about Pa and expressed their hope that he would be alright. We thanked them and assured them that we were confident that Doctor Clark would be able to help.

Just then the good doctor entered Pete's hazy den. We introduced ourselves and assured him that we were ready when he was. "Let's go," He answered anxiously.

We helped the doctor with his black bag into the sleigh. We had brought a blanket for him to sit on and one to cover with. Off we went. The drifting snow had filled the broken banks. That didn't matter to Dick and Barney. Sensing that they were headed home, they plowed through the snow banks with even greater intensity than before. They broke into a gallop, lunging into the drifts with no concern for what they were pulling. My brother quickly tried to rein them in. This wasn't easy since Dick, the friskier of the two, sometimes managed to grab the bit with his teeth. Pull as one might he was off and running at his own pace!

Tipping over would have been a major catastrophe, especially with the doctor aboard. The horses would not have stopped but would have dragged whatever was behind them all the way home. I held my breath a few times as we teetered on one set of runners while the other set caught nothing but air. Doctor Clark sat silently bouncing from side to side leaning into the tipping sleigh with seemingly little or no concern.

Finally, we arrived at our driveway and pulled up in front of our house. We helped Doctor Clark out of the sleigh, taking his arm as he walked into the house. We didn't want him to slip and fall on the hard-packed snow. Once in the house, he wasted no time. With overshoes still on he walked into the living room, removed his gloves, opened his bag and pulled out a syringe and a small vile of medication. He clutched it in his hand for a bit, presumably to warm it some. Finally, he drew some of the adrenalin into the syringe. He warned Pa, "Now this is still a bit cold, so you will feel it." Pa, gasping helplessly for breath, nodded slightly.

Now we all sat and waited. We were confident this would help because this was not the first time we did this. Doctor Clark removed his coat, cap, and overshoes. He apologized for the puddles of water forming on the floor from the melting snow. We invited him to sit awhile. He did. He wanted to be certain that everything was going to be okay with Pa. We thanked the Lord for Doctor Clark. What a blessing to have such a dedicated doctor.

Ma served hot chocolate and cookies and we all engaged in some humorous conversation about the sleigh ride, which Doctor Clark described as "absolutely invigorating," Pa began to gasp less and less and was beginning to breathe more easily.

After Pa's thankful hand shake and Ma's kind words of gratitude, Doctor Clark looked at my brother and me with a twinkle in his eyes and remarked, "Well, are we ready for another one of those inspiring sleigh rides?" We assured him we were and soon we were off. The return trip was not nearly as treacherous since we had made several trips through the snow banks with two plow horses. Once home, Dick and Barney seemed ready for a very long drink of water, a pail of oats each, and a manger full of hay.

The snow continued to drift all night. After three days, the sun came out and temperatures went up into the 20's. Now the real work began. One and a quarter miles of snow banks to shovel by hand with scoop shovels! When we were reasonably sure that the weather had settled down for a while we began working at it. Our neighbors walked by on their way to Pete's Place. They politely asked how Pa was and wished him the best. We thanked them for asking and they were on their way. Sometimes it took a couple of days to shovel out.

Today, I chuckle as I see folks using a snow blower to blow out a driveway of 25 feet! Immediately, I have a flash-back to the "good old days." Snow blizzards were very much a part of our winters as I was growing up in South Dakota. Becoming snowbound for a number of days certainly was not uncommon.

We had learned that life is not made up of simply waiting for the storm to pass. Rather, it is about learning to dance in the snow.

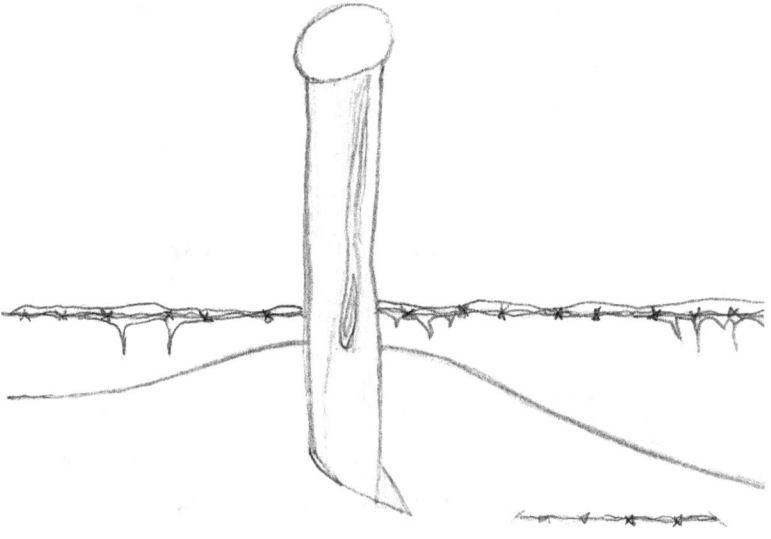

Illustrations by Abby

Words are meant to communicate. Pictures and illustrations are meant to do the same. When words and illustrations are coordinated to communicate thoughts and ideas, as well as tell a story, what a happy marriage results.

It has been said that a picture or illustration is worth a thousand words. It is because we believe this that we are so pleased that Abby graciously took of her time to illustrate the book before you. Her illustrations bring the words to life and vividly fasten the stories in our mind's eye. Without her enjoyable work, this book would not have become what it is.

Abby Matzke, with her husband Philip, are the parents of two preschool children. Of course, they occupy a great deal of Abby's time. Yet she found space to let her imagination soar creating illustrations, which add much to the episodes about growing up in the 30's and 40's in South Dakota.

Abby, also, has performed a yeoman's service in proofing the text and giving helpful advice to promote readability. Her college English major was put to good use.

> Thank you, Abby,
> for your excellent work!
>
> L. Dale Redlin

Growing Up in South Dakota

Many stories could be told or written by those of us who grew up in the South Dakota during the '30s and '40s. Many of them, no doubt, would be rather entertaining and edifying. In fact, I know they would be, because I have heard many. My attempt, however, in this little volume, is to relay episodes from the everyday life of a child growing up in those years to illustrate without exaggeration how life really was in those days.

As I have said on many occasions, I am very thankful to have had the opportunity to grow up during those years in rural South Dakota. When we traveled to Aberdeen, SD, to enroll my sister in college, I wondered if that would ever happen to me. Well, it did. After serving time in the military and continue to farm a few years, I enrolled in the pre-theological course at Bethany Lutheran College and after seven years of theological studies graduated from Immanuel Theological Seminary. I served in the ministry for 40 years and am presently retired.

Hope, my devoted wife of fifty years, has been, indeed, a helper right for me. We have two children and six grandchildren. It was with them in mind that the episodes in this little volume took shape.

It is with deep gratitude for the past and genuine thankfulness for today that we offer this little volume to you.

Yours for some fun reading,

L. Dale Redlin
Abby Matzke, Illustrator

Other Titles by L. Dale Redlin

www.ingramcontent.com/pod-product-compliance
Lightning Source LLC
Chambersburg PA
CBHW071303130626
46556CB00003B/1440